Six Sigma

by Marsha Shapiro and Anthony Weeks

ALPHA
A member of Penguin Group (USA) Inc.

ALPHA BOOKS

Published by the Penguin Group (USA) Inc.

Penguin Group (USA) Inc., 375 Hudson Street, New York, New York 10014, U.S.A.

Penguin Group (Canada), 10 Alcorn Avenue, Toronto, Ontario, Canada M4V 3B2 (a division of Pearson Penguin Canada Inc.)

Penguin Books Ltd, 80 Strand, London WC2R 0RL, England

Penguin Ireland, 25 St Stephen's Green, Dublin 2, Ireland (a division of Penguin Books Ltd)

Penguin Group (Australia), 250 Camberwell Road, Camberwell, Victoria 3124, Australia (a division of Pearson Australia Group Pty Ltd)

Penguin Books India Pvt Ltd, 11 Community Centre, Panchsheel Park, New Delhi—110 017, India

Penguin Group (NZ), cnr Airborne and Rosedale Roads, Albany, Auckland 1310, New Zealand (a division of Pearson New Zealand Ltd)

Penguin Books (South Africa) (Pty) Ltd, 24 Sturdee Avenue, Rosebank, Johannesburg 2196, South Africa

Penguin Books Ltd, Registered Offices: 80 Strand, London WC2R 0RL, England

International Standard Book Number: 1-59257-422-X
Library of Congress Catalog Card Number: 2005929449

07 06 05 8 7 6 5 4 3 2 1

Interpretation of the printing code: The rightmost number of the first series of numbers is the year of the book's printing; the rightmost number of the second series of numbers is the number of the book's printing. For example, a printing code of 05-1 shows that the first printing occurred in 2005.

Printed in the United States of America

Note: This publication contains the opinions and ideas of its authors. It is intended to provide helpful and informative material on the subject matter covered. It is sold with the understanding that the authors and publisher are not engaged in rendering professional services in the book. If the reader requires personal assistance or advice, a competent professional should be consulted.

The authors and publisher specifically disclaim any responsibility for any liability, loss, or risk, personal or otherwise, which is incurred as a consequence, directly or indirectly, of the use and application of any of the contents of this book.

Contents

Introduction

Six Sigma, a data-based process improvement methodology, is a term popping up everywhere. The adoption of Six Sigma is spreading throughout all types and sizes of companies. From manufacturing to service industries, CEOs are recognizing the benefits of using Six Sigma and, in most cases, are driving the infiltration.

Within the companies embracing Six Sigma, every employee is ultimately affected. If you work for a company that is about to adopt Six Sigma, or is in the early stage of investigating its effectiveness, this book will help you understand the practice, implementation, and successes related to a Six Sigma implementation.

What's Inside

The Pocket Idiot's Guide to Six Sigma provides insight into understanding where Six Sigma originated, as well as how and why it has grown so much in popularity in such a short period of time. You will find straightforward explanations about how people, data, projects, and organizational structures lead to solving business problems throughout an organization.

Here's what you'll find in this book.

Chapter 1, "Six Sigma Explained," provides a brief overview of Six Sigma along with the history of how it began. You will also get real-life examples of how companies are using Six Sigma to achieve real benefits.

Chapter 2, "Why Six Sigma?," compares Six Sigma to other process-improvement methodologies used today. You'll also understand how Six Sigma becomes a corporate philosophy and way of life as it uses data to make decisions, along with a structured project approach to implementation.

Chapter 3, "The Technique," details the steps used by Six Sigma to define, analyze, measure, improve, and control the problem.

Chapter 4, "The Tool Belt," addresses the common set of tools used throughout the Six Sigma project. You will also learn how to use these tools outside of a Six Sigma project to fix things that might be broken in your particular area.

Chapter 5, "Belts That Fit," talks about the structure of an organization as it adopts Six Sigma. In this chapter, you will learn the roles involved in successfully implementing a Six Sigma program, along with the selection process required to effectively fill these roles.

Chapter 6, "Living with Change," focuses on the management of changes resulting from Six Sigma implementations. We will talk about the human side of change and how to head off conflict before it arises.

Chapter 7, "Join in the Fun," prepares you for joining a team. You'll find out what is expected from team members and what team members should expect from the team lead.

Chapter 8, "Accepting the Lead," helps you decide when and if you might be ready to take on a larger role in a Six Sigma organization. You'll find out what characteristics you need to become a lead and what your future might look like if you take this opportunity.

Chapter 9, "Creative Solutions," provides an overview of alternative processes used in a Six Sigma organization. You'll learn what happens when new processes are required and how to find quick results while longer-term solutions are being addressed.

Chapter 10, "Going Astray," will keep you abreast of what can go wrong in a Six Sigma organization. In this chapter you will hear about common mistakes and how to avoid them.

Appendix A contains a Sigma values table, and Appendix B provides definitions for the key terms used in the book.

Featured Information

Throughout this book you will also find three types of sidebar boxes to improve your understanding of Six Sigma.

Process Pointers

Here you'll find tips to make the process of implementing Six Sigma go easier.

Sigma Sayings

These boxes contain definitions of key terms used to describe Six Sigma.

Defect Alert

These boxes list common problems you might run into, along with how to avoid them.

Acknowledgments

This book was most definitely a team effort, and we want to thank the people at Alpha books for their patience and guidance throughout the process, particularly acquisitions editor Mike Sanders.

Marsha wants to give particular thanks to her sister, Debra Gordon, for bringing this project to her attention and providing support and encouragement throughout. Most important, she thanks her ever-loving husband, Adam, along with her three children, Jordan, Hannah, and Max, for exuding complete patience, support, and excitement during the many hours spent writing this book.

Tony sends a warm thanks to his dad, Don Weeks, for introducing him to Six Sigma at Motorola back in 1988.

Trademarks

All terms mentioned in this book that are known to be or are suspected of being trademarks or service marks have been appropriately capitalized. Alpha Books and Penguin Group (USA) Inc. cannot attest to the accuracy of this information. Use of a term in this book should not be regarded as affecting the validity of any trademark or service mark.

Chapter 1

Six Sigma Explained

In This Chapter

- A basic explanation of Six Sigma
- The origins of Six Sigma
- Why you should understand the philosophy
- How companies have adopted the Six Sigma approach

Your neighbor just told you he was asked to lead a Six Sigma green belt project. Your boss requires you to sign up for Six Sigma overview training. Flipping through the classifieds, you see a position for a Six Sigma black belt. All you currently know about Sigma is that it's a Greek letter. All you know about black belts is what you learned in karate class or from Bruce Lee films. What does all this mean, and what does it have to do with business?

In this book, we explain the Six Sigma philosophy and why it continues to grow in popularity among corporate executives, managers, supervisors, and employees. You'll understand how companies are improving bottom-line results using the Six Sigma tools and techniques. By comparing Six Sigma with other problem-solving approaches, you will see Six Sigma as a true corporate philosophy rather than an exercise in training. Finally, we'll arm you with ideas for becoming a more effective employee as we provide real-life examples of Six Sigma successes along with simple, clever ways to make improvements in your company.

A Moment of Clarity

Six Sigma is a structured methodology used by businesses to improve the way they do things. By focusing in on the things that are broken and identifying just how broken they are, companies are able to find and implement solutions quickly.

The Process

If you are new to the corporate world, you may be surprised to find out that no company is perfect. Companies continuously try to improve the way they operate by fixing the way things work or by fixing their internal *processes*.

Sigma Sayings

Process refers to a string of actions focused toward a goal or end result. Examples of processes include cooking dinner, answering a phone, or building airplanes.

Processes are all around you. You will find processes in your daily job, company, and personal life. Processes are simply the steps you take to get something accomplished. For instance, companies have processes for paying insurance claims, answering help desk calls, and manufacturing aircrafts. In fact, you follow a process when you get dressed every morning. Some of the steps in your process might include:

- Selecting clothes to wear
- Taking off pajamas
- Putting on clothes
- Brushing teeth
- Putting on socks
- Putting on shoes

While you might be satisfied with the end result of being dressed, not all processes always achieve the desired goal. For instance, maybe one day you find that you are taking too long to get dressed. The next day you might change or fix your process to select your clothes the night before in order to eliminate this step from your morning process.

Sigma Sayings

A **goal** is the targeted end result, which may or may not be achieved, due to various factors.

When companies fix processes, they hope to achieve reduced costs, increased sales, shorter time to market, or anything that ultimately increases customer satisfaction. Even charitable organizations strive to do better, resulting in increased aid for their represented cause.

The Customer

Six Sigma will help identify processes that are not functioning appropriately. When we say a process is not functioning appropriately, we mean the output or end result produced by the process does not meet the expectation of the *customer*.

Sigma Sayings

A **customer** is someone receiving the output or end result of your process.

For instance, assume your friend follows the same process as you to get dressed every morning. Your friend may believe that the 20 minutes it takes to complete the process of getting dressed is perfectly acceptable. But, if you believe you should complete the process in 10 minutes, you will need to modify your process to meet the expectation of *your* customer—you! The output of your process (20 minutes to get dressed) is unacceptable and must be fixed.

Focusing on the customer's expectation requires you to know who your customer is. For instance, if your process is to sell hamburgers, your customer is the person buying the hamburger. If your process is to read a book to your daughter's class, your customers are the children in your daughter's class.

ALERT

Defect Alert

If you don't know who your customers are and completely understand what they want, you won't be able to produce goods or services to their satisfaction.

In many cases, your customer might be another functional area within the same company. We call this an internal customer. For instance, the customers for a corporate help line might be store associates. Customers for an aircraft engine crew might be the pilots or engineers.

Variation

After finding your customer, the next step to understanding Six Sigma is to understand *variation*. Consider the example of driving to work. Some days, the trip takes you 20 minutes, some days it takes 23 minutes, and some days it takes 25 minutes. Each day the time needed to travel the same distance can vary. The goal of Six Sigma is to understand and reduce or eliminate this variation in a business context.

Sigma Sayings

Variation refers to something happening that is different from that which was expected. It is the fluctuation in the process output or the spread of data around the process mean, sometimes called *noise*.

For instance, one reason for the variation for your drive to work might be traffic. Another reason might be the number of red lights you hit. Perhaps the variation in travel time is due to the time of day you left your house. By identifying "travel time" as the goal (that is, 20 minutes), which was established by your customer (you), and by analyzing potential causes for lateness (such as traffic, red lights, and time of day), you might find that leaving the house every day at a specific time allows you to travel with less traffic and thus reduce variation in your arrival time. The end result would be a satisfied customer, including you, your boss, and your employees!

Another example to understand variation might be the variation in the cycle time for processing a purchase requisition. Sometimes, purchase requisitions are signed and processed quickly, while at other times the requisition might require additional signatures, the signees might be out on vacation, or the vendor does not reply with the proper terms.

All of these factors might create variation in the processing time of a purchase requisition.

Eliminate the Gut Feel

So why did your company have to adopt Six Sigma to eliminate variation in processes? Aren't there enough smart people just like you to help reduce costs and satisfy customers? Unfortunately, even smart people sometimes make the wrong decisions when not enough information is available. Or perhaps your experience has biased you to think you know the solution or process modifications when, in fact, you are missing the critical cause of the process issues. Six Sigma focuses on making sure the right level of information exists to solve the problem at hand.

Suppose your company produces and sells one million widgets each year, and each year half of the widgets are faulty and returned by your customers. A typical response might be to make recommendations based on your life experiences in the production of widgets. You might suggest that the machine age is a factor in producing problem widgets. As a result, you recommend your company purchase new machinery and train operators on the new equipment. After spending a significant amount of money, you determine the problem still exists. We like to refer to this common scenario as the *Gut Feel* approach.

Defect Alert

Using Six Sigma helps companies avoid using the Gut Feel approach in problem solving, which is usually non-factual and results in making changes to an organization that do not solve the business problem.

Using the Six Sigma approach to solving the widget issue, you might gather a team together made up of factory floor workers, production supervisors, returns processing associates, logistics folks, salespeople, and customers. Your team would work together, using their varying perspectives, to identify how your customers expect the widget to perform. Based on this information, you and your team are able to clearly define what is meant by a faulty widget. Faulty widgets are sometimes an output of the process of manufacturing widgets. In Six Sigma, these faulty widgets are considered *defects* because they do not meet the customer's quality expectations.

Sigma Sayings

A **defect** is an error or mistake resulting in reduced customer satisfaction.

Using the tools and techniques inherent within the Six Sigma methodology, your team would begin the process of fixing the widget problem by ensuring the method of counting customer returns is accurate and consistent throughout your company. Once the customer returns data is validated, your team will have an accurate picture of how many substandard products your widget production process is producing.

Next, your team would research all potential causes for the defective widgets. By selecting and analyzing the one or two key causes that have the greatest potential impact on eliminating or reducing the number of returned widgets, your team would recommend and test changes to reduce or eliminate the causes. After testing the solution to ensure your desired results are achieved, you would be ready to implement.

With the rigor of the Six Sigma structure, you can reduce the risk of implementing costly solutions that don't solve the problem.

A Statistical Approach

Achieving the right level of quality is another reason companies turn to Six Sigma. Based on your company and the outputs it produces, you might find that certain processes come close enough to meeting customer expectations to be okay. Oftentimes, however, employees continue to spend time and money trying to make these processes better.

Six Sigma helps your company decide what to fix and what not to fix. How close to perfection should you go? How much perfection can you afford?

The Six Sigma approach uses *statistics* to generate a standard quality measure. It focuses on shifting existing quality toward the predefined standard.

Sigma Sayings

Statistics refers to a mathematical system used to understand a larger segment (population) of data by analyzing a sample or small portion of the data.

Companies using Six Sigma are able to quantify quality. This provides them the ability to evaluate more easily when and where improvements are required. They do this by applying a quality measure, or sigma value, to every process.

Sigma, the Greek symbol Σ, is a statistical term used to explain how much variation exists relative to customer expectations. A 6.0 Sigma process (or *Six Sigma*) has very little variation. Specifically, if you were producing one million widgets, and only three or four widgets were returned by customers, the resulting sigma level would be at or near 6.0. Nearly perfect!

Sigma Sayings

Six Sigma refers to a management philosophy adopted throughout all areas of an organization that is used to solve business problems. The term Six Sigma also refers to a quality measure (that is, 3.4 defects per 1 million chances or opportunities is 6.0 Sigma). The fewer defects produced, the higher sigma level and quality achieved.

Just as all people are not perfect, not every business process will be perfect. In most cases, the cost of achieving perfection outweighs the return. If you understand your customers' expectations, you will be able to get as close to perfection as possible without losing value. Understanding what makes your customer happy will determine what level of sigma is acceptable for your process.

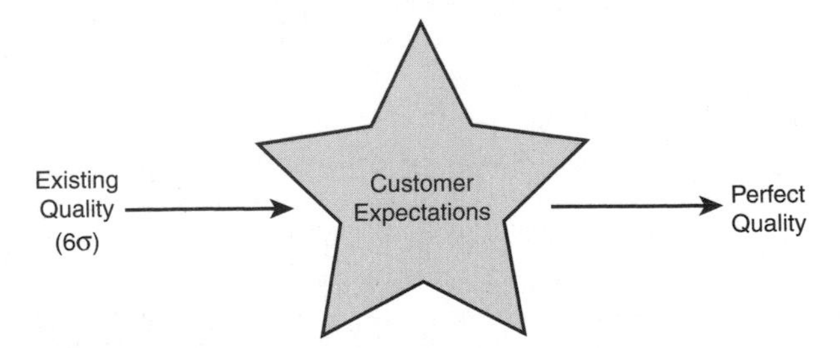

The road toward perfection starts and ends with customer expectations.

To better understand why a company might or might not need to achieve perfect quality, consider a company that produces heart monitors. The process resulting in the output of heart monitors will require a much higher sigma level than a process resulting in answering calls for a call center. Of course, if the call center is 911 emergency response, a near perfect sigma level would be expected.

Origin and Adoption

Understanding how Six Sigma began will provide you with insight into why companies like yours are interested in adopting it.

Six Sigma was first used in the business world beginning in the mid 1980s by engineers at Motorola. Their goal was to improve quality by implementing a common method of counting defects. By capturing a *baseline*, they found that significant increases in performance could be achieved by making improvements necessary to meet customer expectations.

Sigma Sayings

Baseline refers to a historical measurement of the current process output that may be used as a comparison to customer expectations.

As employees at Motorola began to see improvements in quality with movements from low sigma levels to 3–5Σ, they began to spread the practice across all facets of the organization. By the late 1980s to early 1990s, a Motorola architect, Mikel Harry, founded the Six Sigma Academy in an effort to involve companies such as Allied, IBM, and Kodak in expanding and perfecting the Six Sigma process.

One of the most notable adopters of Six Sigma was General Electric. Under Jack Welch's leadership, GE is credited for turning Six Sigma into a way of life for employees and suppliers. He encouraged every resource to find better ways to do their jobs. High savings goals were set throughout the company forcing the use of Six Sigma to achieve these targets.

As GE began to publish the hundreds of millions of dollars in savings resulting from successful Six Sigma implementations, other companies began to investigate and adopt this methodology. While the growth began in manufacturing, today, industries such as banking, retail, software, and medical all have companies successfully using Six Sigma.

Whether you work for a manufacturing or a services company, you should know that Six Sigma can and has been used to improve processes throughout operations, sales, marketing, information technology, finance, and even human resources.

Getting Started

If your company is thinking about adopting Six Sigma, you might wonder how easy of a task this will be. As with the implementation of any new methodology or corporate practice, getting started can present many challenges.

Usually, the decision to bring in Six Sigma comes from the top. Your CEO or top-level executive probably read about the savings achieved at other companies and decided to get started. If this is the case, you have little to worry about. However, if the idea originated from a lower-level employee and complete acceptance at the executive level is not achieved, Six Sigma implementations can fail.

Unfortunately, as an employee you may not feel the pain of Six Sigma failure until a project touches your area with under-committed or under-supported resources resulting in poorly implemented solutions.

Process Pointers

If you are making the recommendation to bring Six Sigma into your company, begin by finding an executive champion. Leverage this champion to spread the adoption of Six Sigma throughout the executive level.

Another challenge companies like yours face when adopting Six Sigma is how to introduce it after acceptance is achieved. A company starting Six Sigma is required to make tough choices. Should they buy it, build it, or both?

The buy-it approach requires a large up-front dollar investment to bring in permanent resources with advanced Six Sigma knowledge to drive and implement improvements in critical business areas. Alternatively, the build-it approach uses existing resources and requires an investment in training and materials.

The combination of buy-it and build-it blends the best of both worlds by bringing in consultants to train, jumpstart, and manage the program while growing talent internally.

Process Pointers

If a company is tasked with starting a Six Sigma program, it must understand the dollar investment and timeframe requirements before selecting an approach.

The Buy-It Approach

Hiring experienced *black belts* and *master black belts* (detailed in Chapter 5) into an organization can often get the program up and running faster than training current employees.

Sigma Sayings

Black belt refers to a full-time Six Sigma project leader. **Master black belt** identifies a full-time trainer and mentor of Six Sigma usually responsible for overseeing the implementation of Six Sigma throughout the entire organization.

Results can be achieved more quickly by hiring black belts and having them start working on projects immediately—eliminating the need for lengthy Six Sigma training. Still, companies need to provide training to their black belts on their business strategies and cultural benefits.

Drawbacks to the approach of hiring black belts and master black belts include the up-front expenses and the associated risks of hiring new employees. Companies will have to ensure the new belts will be a good fit in their organizations and can command the respect required to spearhead improvements. Often, a new resource is faced with resistance from team members due to lack of experience and knowledge of the functional area.

Companies also might run into a lack of commitment from the top. While the CEO may be gung-ho about Six Sigma, do his direct reports feel the same way? Will new employees have the clout needed to convince upper management that Six Sigma is worth hearing about? This knowledge transfer is critical to the sustainability of a Six Sigma program.

Process Pointers

Companies that decide to bring in black belt project leaders from the outside should be sure to have a training program defined to help the new hire quickly understand the business knowledge.

The good news about the buy-it approach is that, if successfully implemented, a company can usually begin recognizing savings quickly. Some of the savings realized can go into offsetting the up-front hiring expenses. We also see organizations adopt the best practices when bringing in experienced Six Sigma leaders rather than cultivating their own.

The Build-It Approach

If an organization has a strong culture and typically promotes from within, it might want to consider the build-it approach. This usually requires the company to bring in a consultant temporarily to help jumpstart the program. Involvement from the outside can be as simple as helping to create training materials to as complicated as organizing an entire selection process (discussed in Chapter 5), including interviewing and selection.

Typical expenses include the consulting services and licensing of materials. Taking this road can often lead to lengthy project schedules as black belts familiarize themselves with the process.

Defect Alert

When selecting consultants to create materials or administer initial training, make certain a seasoned employee is heavily involved to ensure that the materials make sense for your company and industry.

The best part about the build-it approach is teaching people already familiar with your current processes how to make improvements. Because these new belts are typically selected because they are highly respected in their current roles, they will have the drive and passion to preach Six Sigma to their co-workers, bosses, direct reports, and peers across the organization. Sit back and watch as they spread the word.

The Combo

We actually recommend that most companies combine the build-it and buy-it approaches when starting a new Six Sigma program. By bringing in experienced master black belts focused on the training and coaching of existing resources, projects can begin quickly. This sets a solid foundation of pairing business knowledge with Six Sigma expertise, resulting in a Six Sigma program with strong roots that spread throughout the organization.

Real-Life Examples

Now you are ready for us to show you the money. But what if we tell you it's not always about saving money? As we discussed previously, Six Sigma is all about making improvements—improving processes that result in greater customer satisfaction. When customers are satisfied, companies do better. Sometimes these improvements result in immediate savings, but sometimes the benefits are projected to be realized in the future. For instance, if you make your customers happy now, they may buy more of your products or services later.

Projects aimed at reducing costs, such as payroll or operational costs, often lead to *hard-dollar savings*. Some companies require a certain percentage of Six Sigma projects to focus on these hard-dollar savings in order to show an immediate effect on the bottom line. Alternately, some projects focus on soft-dollar savings, such as increasing sales or avoiding costs in the future. Regardless of the benefit structure, the end results are still the same. Both project types produce process improvements that satisfy customer needs, resulting in higher market share and, ultimately, improved margins.

Sigma Sayings

Hard-dollar savings refers to expenses eliminated from a company's budget, such as reduced payroll expenses or reduced energy costs.

In the following sections, we discuss real-world examples of Six Sigma improvements achieved across various organizations.

The Faster the Better

A major medical company fills 80,000 mail order prescriptions per day. The company used to spend a great deal of time and effort ensuring each prescription was accurately filled. This *purchased accuracy* (attempt to buy quality) was done by having a series of multiple inspectors check the same prescriptions. If a prescription ships incorrectly or does not include accurate information on potential interactions with other drugs, a patient could be harmed.

The Six Sigma process improvement project started with using a measurement analysis to determine whether the extra inspections really added value. The study first showed that only a small percentage of the prescriptions had a potentially significant reaction with other medications. The question came down to: "Why do the maximum inspection on all products when only 20 percent need the critical inspection?" Through further analysis, the company found few defects were caught by the last inspector. This was attributed to the recent, successful implementation of a new bottling process wherein the drug information was added to the prescription earlier in the process as opposed to the pharmacist adding the facts at the end of the process.

Using additional statistical analysis tools and structured testing processes, the company concluded that only 60 percent of the original verification process was required. The prescriptions were shipped more quickly because one inspection step was eliminated for the critical prescriptions and two inspections were eliminated for the noncritical prescriptions.

Through the implementation of this new "prescription check" verification system, the company was able to reduce the number of inspections, and, as a result, reduce the time required to verify, ship, and mail a prescription.

Unpaid Bills

A large printer of phone books had an issue with some of its customers not paying their invoices. Using Six Sigma, the printer found that the nonpayment was due to distorted photographs within the customers' ads on the pages of the phone book. The Six Sigma effort found that after many consecutive runs of the printing press, the color would have a tendency to shift and result in a blurring or smearing of the photographic images.

To solve this defect, the printing press set-up and product-run processes were modified to include color alignment samples and check points. Simply put, a color target system was added to the front, middle, and back sections of the phone book to be used as process-control measures. Samples were pulled at the beginning of each run to verify set-up, and then randomly throughout the print job, to verify that the print alignment was accurate or on target. If a misalignment was found, the defect could be caught and corrected before a large number of books were produced.

As a result of this improvement, the company was able to collect nearly 100 percent of payments on all future work.

Good Enough to Eat

The manufacturer of the white pigment in M&Ms (which is between the chocolate and the candy shell) had an issue with washing the pigment to make it bright white. The manufacturer used several wash cycles with partially recycled cleaning solutions. The analysis found that by using recycled cleaning solutions, the pigment could not be cleaned to satisfactory quality levels.

Through the implementation of full-strength cleaning solutions, this manufacturer was able to achieve the highest level of cleanliness with a reduced number of cycles. These results led to less waste along with a reduced cycle time. These savings far outweighed the cost of using the full-strength cleaning solutions. More importantly, this company saved the customer from abandoning their product.

And We'll Tell Two Friends

A major kitchen installer had an issue with customers not recommending them to friends or relatives. In a survey asking "Would you recommend us (the installer) to your friend?" the reply of "yes" was less than 15 percent. Additional survey questions found that customer perceptions of the kitchen installs were negative. Customers felt the installs were taking too long, or longer than promised. In reality, the cabinet-ordering cycle time was taking three weeks—the install time was three days.

As a result, the project focused on reducing the time required to fill the cabinet order. After reducing the cabinet-ordering cycle time from three weeks to three days, the company found that customers were now more likely to recommend their services.

The potential sales growth of retaining current or gaining new customers through referrals would allow for a potential of nearly $1 million in additional annual sales.

The Least You Need to Know

- Six Sigma is a structured approach to solving business problems.
- Sigma describes the amount of variation in a process output compared to customer expectations.
- Outputs of a process that fall below customer expectations are called "defects."
- Greater sigma levels mean higher quality and fewer defects.
- Six Sigma began in the mid 1980s at Motorola and has since expanded, thriving across many different types of organizations.
- Making customers happy is the big payoff resulting from a successful Six Sigma implementation.

Why Six Sigma?

In This Chapter

- A comparison across quality improvement programs
- Six Sigma as a corporate way of life
- Project roles
- Understanding the importance of project management
- Why data drives improvements

While companies adopt Six Sigma as a direct solution to solving problems, consulting firms, training organizations, and placement services are recognizing this initiative as a new market for products and services. But, let's face it, Six Sigma is not the first methodology to talk about improving quality and saving money. You might work for a company that has adopted standards in the past with supporters boasting exactly the same benefits. If so, you're now wondering if Six Sigma is simply another fad backed by popular demand.

In this chapter, we discuss why Six Sigma has jumped to the top of the pack of process-improvement methodologies as we compare it to other quality-improvement approaches. And, by exploring the management and project structure—along with the unique use of data, which is inherent in this philosophy—you'll see why Six Sigma is here to stay.

Comparatively Speaking

So, what did companies do before Six Sigma? How were problems solved? Your company may have solved problems using pieces of Six Sigma without even knowing it. It might have learned about these tools and processes from other programs adopted in the past. In fact, your company might still be using other quality initiatives today as it makes the decision to move into the world of Six Sigma.

We like to think of Six Sigma as the umbrella of all other quality initiatives. Many of the Six Sigma tools were actually around long before Motorola engineers introduced the approach. However, most other quality initiatives only use these tools sparingly and independent of one another to solve problems. In fact, other quality initiatives have much smaller toolkits and rely on the Gut Feel approach, which we described in Chapter 1. Six Sigma pulls the best of the best together to create a complete business solution.

Quality, Quality, Quality

Total Quality Management (TQM), one of the most popular quality methodologies, is a collection of tools that helps an assembly line manager or production manager run a shop floor. We would also describe TQM as an organized way for identifying and fixing easy-to-solve problems. Charts for tracking production along with work-out sessions are techniques commonly used to get as many people involved in identifying the right solution.

TQM, by far, is the most tool-driven methodology next to Six Sigma. The major difference we find between TQM and Six Sigma is the lack of math or statistical tools used to prove solutions prior to implementation. Instead, TQM primarily uses experience and popularity voting. Tools such as multi-voting, cause-and-effect diagrams, and failure modes and effects analysis are used for selecting the correct solutions. In most cases, the users of TQM will use manual control charting techniques to monitor the process after a solution has been implemented.

I Do Declare

Another widely recognized quality program is the ISO9000 quality series initiatives including 9001 and 9014. These initiatives were developed by the International Standards Organization (ISO) as a way to document the work being done by manufacturers to ensure quality management.

This is a good method to use prior to implementing Six Sigma, mostly because this methodology requires you, as an employee, to document your critical processes.

Process Pointers

The International Standards Organization, a group focused on creating and maintaining worldwide standards for quality assurance procedures, does *not* regulate or ensure product quality. Keep this in mind when looking at ISO-certified processes. Instead, the ISO simply requires that companies formalize and keep quality assurance and reporting procedures in place and meet specific standards as defined by the organization. If you produce a defective product, the ISO will not correct the procedure used to produce it; it only documents the defect.

The ISO method of documentation often has companies viewing their processes from the 10,000-foot level. An examination at this level often results in missing broken steps, for example, steps that overlook inefficiencies or redundancies.

For example, the ISO process map for a check-out process may be as follows:

1. Take product out of cart.
2. Scan item.

3. Demagnetize sensormatic strip.
4. Check screen to see if item rang up.
5. Place item in bag.
6. Place bag in cart.

The real process steps would include the broken steps as follows:

1. Take item out of cart.
2. Identify UPC.
3. If no UPC exists, look up item in book.
4. If no item in book, call for assistance on price check.
5. Key in item.
6. Verify correct item keyed in.
7. Verify correct price.
8. Demagnetize sensormatic strip.
9. Are bags available?
10. If bags are unavailable, find bags.
11. Place product in bag.
12. Place bag in cart.

Believe it or not, an ISO certification can be achieved without making improvements to your process. The only requirement for certification is that a company's processes are well-documented, not necessarily well-conceived. For this reason, many companies are moving away from ISO and implementing a more results-focused approach like Six Sigma.

And the Award Goes to ...

Another word that often comes up during a discussion about quality is *Baldridge*. This term actually refers to the Malcolm Baldridge National Quality Award. This is an award given by the president of the United States to businesses that apply—they must be in manufacturing or service, but they can be small or large companies. The businesses are assessed in seven areas and must be judged as outstanding in all areas to be awarded. If your company has strived to win the Baldridge award in the past, they worked hard to excel in the following areas:

- Leadership
- Strategic planning
- Customer and market focus
- Measurement, analysis, and knowledge management
- Human resources focus
- Process management
- Results

The award originated to encourage American companies, based on the renewed need for quality, as an effort to remain competitive in the expanding global market. However, the Baldridge award does not recommend specific tools to use. It only recommends certification requirements and end results. How the results are achieved is up to the companies participating in the award process.

Motorola was the first company to win the award in 1988. By pulling together some of the TQM tools they were currently utilizing to conform to the Baldridge criteria, and by targeting efforts on specific issues rather than generic strategies, Six Sigma was born.

A Management Philosophy

Six Sigma achieves such a high number of successes because it employs a holistic approach to action. While the decision to bring in Six Sigma usually comes from the top, the practice of Six Sigma affects everyone in the organization. We strongly believe that when any one level of the company is excluded from employing Six Sigma, the whole company's chance of victory is at risk.

The Sponsor

Let's start with your CEO or top executive. This is the person who sets the direction in your company and, consequently, is the one who will jump-start the adoption of Six Sigma as the company's approach to solving business problems. But spearheading the adoption of the Six Sigma philosophy is not where the CEO's role ends. In fact, to ensure the victory and sustainability of the overall program, the CEO must have an on-going role from project selection to completion.

Most Six Sigma projects are aimed at fixing broken processes. But how does a company like yours find what is broken? When a CEO establishes clear metrics (goals) based on customer expectations and that metric is not achieved, the CEO begins to look for the cause of the problem by looking at the process producing the metric or output. Chances are they will find a broken process.

Defect Alert

When companies lack definitive corporate goals aligned at the executive level, acknowledging the existence of problems and attaining support to fix them will not occur.

For example, suppose an executive in your company is rated annually on how quickly the company restocks merchandise, also known as the rate of inventory turns. If the metric was defined as 30 turns per year, but the actual number of inventory turns for the year was only 20, the executive would begin to investigate the inventory processes to determine which process was causing the lower inventory turns. Without an executive being held accountable for inventory turns, this problem might be overlooked until a more serious problem results.

Even though your executive might have found a broken process, why should he focus resources to get it fixed? One major reason is that executive bonus structures and performance reviews are usually tied to metrics. This encourages executives to find solutions quickly. If the CEO in charge of inventory turns expects to receive a bonus for exceeding 30 turns per year, he is more likely to watch this metric closely throughout the year to prevent negative year-end results.

The Champions

If the CEO has effectively persuaded the rest of the executives that Six Sigma can solve problems quickly, they will use Six Sigma to fix the processes (or problems) in their respective areas.

As the executive or corporate-level metrics filter down to middle management, the mid-level managers now have a stake in fixing the problems. Suppose inventory turns were tracked by region and each regional manager had an individual goal based on the established corporate goal. The executive in charge of inventory turns can look directly to the region or regions where turns are at risk and demand action. Because these regional managers were given clear inventory turn objectives at the beginning of the year, they too have a stake in fixing the problem quickly.

Even after project selection, executives in a Six Sigma organization are not done. They now move into the project champion role. As the top-level project supporters, these champions set direction and eliminate roadblocks. The champions will also assist in ensuring appropriate resources are committed for the duration of the project.

Process Pointers

Project selection must be aligned with corporate strategy to ensure it receives dedication from team members, sponsors, and process participants. Align projects to key executive metrics and ensure the executive owning the success metric is identified up front as the project sponsor for the Six Sigma initiative. When corporate strategies are vague, projects may begin to overlap or conflict, resulting in a lack of critical resources and direction, both of which are required to complete a project.

Without a committed project champion, most Six Sigma projects will fail. This role is the most important in achieving Six Sigma success. Project champions are responsible for:

- Selecting projects aligned with corporate objectives
- Assigning resources
- Approving project direction
- Eliminating roadblocks

When a project champion is removed from a project prior to completion, a new champion must be assigned immediately to continue the momentum of the project.

The Lead

After a project has been defined, a project leader, or belt, is assigned to lead the project. While the champion owns ultimate responsibility for the project, the belt gets the project done. Similar to the world of karate, the color name prefix of the belt usually determines the level of training received and may dictate the type of project a belt will lead.

Black belts are typically assigned to manage multiple projects simultaneously or partner with other black belts to complete larger projects. One major difference between black belts and other color belts is that black belts lead Six Sigma projects full-time. This dedication enables total focus on using the Six Sigma tools and methodology to solve business problems.

Another difference between black belts and lower-level belts is that black belts usually receive more in-depth training in the Six Sigma tools and methodology. This provides the opportunity to use more sophisticated tools for solving problems. Because a black belt's projects are usually the most complex of any Six Sigma projects, the more tools and knowledge acquired, the more successful results will be achieved.

After a champion assigns a black belt to a project, the black belt's job begins by ensuring the problem is clearly defined. The black belt works with the champion to convert the problem statement into a Six Sigma project definition based on skills acquired in training.

Next, the black belt is responsible for ensuring that the project is properly resourced. This begins with the selection of knowledgeable team members. In conjunction with the project sponsor or project champion, the black belt must identify the individuals who understand the area and process with which the problem is associated. Because a black belt continues to lead the project, the following skills are required:

- The know-how to lead a team effectively
- A comprehensive understanding of the Six Sigma principals
- The ability to utilize the Six Sigma tool set to solve problems

Similar to a black belt, a *green belt* is responsible for leading Six Sigma projects that are typically smaller in scope and within their area of influence or focus. A green belt continues to perform his or her regular job while attacking a particular business problem using the Six Sigma technique. The area of focus for a green belt is usually the area in which they currently work.

Sigma Sayings

Green belt refers to a part-time Six Sigma project leader who usually focuses on smaller projects while performing another job in the company. A green belt is commonly assigned to fix problems within the functional area to which they report.

The following is an example to help you understand how valuable green belts can be:

> An officer of a major company needed to reduce telecommunications spending by $30 million. Data identified four major areas where cost was exceeding planned spending: long distance, data lines, pagers, and line transfers. The officer put the process owner over each of these areas through green belt training with the expectation that they would focus on their individual areas, complete the process improvements, and collectively deliver the desired project savings.

While green belts need a basic understanding of the Six Sigma methodology, their practical knowledge of the tool set is often limited. In some cases, green belts will partner with more experienced belts when certain statistical tools are required. The primary skills required for a green belt are a strong understanding of the business area in which the problem exists along with knowledge of a few basic tools that aid in successfully completing a project.

Some companies have adopted additional color-coded roles such as orange belts and yellow belts to encourage problem-solving throughout the organization. Again, smaller amounts of training are provided along with less-stringent project completion requirements.

Process Pointers

After just a few days of orange belt training, a store manager identified vacuum cleaner sales were 92 percent below market sales. By applying just one of the Six Sigma tools learned in class, the orange belt found product placement to be at fault. As a result, a 240 percent sales increase was achieved by resetting the merchandise.

Again, the main goal of an organization implementing Six Sigma is to deliver the message to as many people in the organization as possible. By learning just a few simple tools and using the basic principles of Six Sigma to implement project solutions, benefits can be achieved throughout every facet of a company. If you add up all these benefits, the return on investment can be huge!

The Trainer

Training the organization is often the most difficult task associated with implementing the Six Sigma methodology. Many companies set goals for the percentage of employees they want to gain some level of Six Sigma understanding. A master black belt is responsible for spreading Six Sigma knowledge both inside and outside a classroom setting.

Spreading Six Sigma knowledge throughout the organization consists of …

- Training the organization at all levels.
- Setting goals and objectives for the operational aspects of Six Sigma within an organization.
- Mentoring other belts.
- Managing more complex Six Sigma projects.

Master black belts are typically in charge of all belt-learning activities. In rare cases, companies will utilize master trainers or advanced black belts to do the training. When this occurs, a master black belt is typically present for sharing application and project examples in addition to acting as the application expert.

Classroom training can vary from 4 to 5 weeks for black belts to a few hours for an executive overview. The amount of time spent in the classroom is a direct correlation to how Six Sigma will be used by the participant following training. By creating this role-based training, master black belts can help reduce training expenses and realize quicker returns.

Master black belts are often tasked with the continued success of Six Sigma throughout an organization. To accomplish this, a master black belt must wear many hats, including advisor, coach, and project coordinator. Master black belts usually partner with an executive in charge of Six Sigma to set project goals and organizational training objectives.

Process Pointers

Master black belts usually have many years of experience successfully leading black belt projects and demonstrating expert knowledge of the Six Sigma toolkit. This creates a valuable resource for developing and executing training curriculum.

Finally, you will find master black belts creating and maintaining the structure for the Six Sigma organization. In some companies, black belts report directly to functional executives to which their projects belong. Other companies prefer a direct reporting structure into a Six Sigma operational group with indirect reporting to the functional executive. This operational group is usually managed by master black belts. In either reporting structure, the master black belt will play a major role in the development and future success of the other belts in the organization.

The Team

No project leader is expected to solve the problem alone. Without the right team, a project will fail. Team members are selected based on their knowledge of the business area in which the problem exists. The team is created to *solve* the business problem. This means the team defines and implements the solution. When the project leader has completed the project, many of these team members continue to support the new process as existing members of the functional area to which the process belongs.

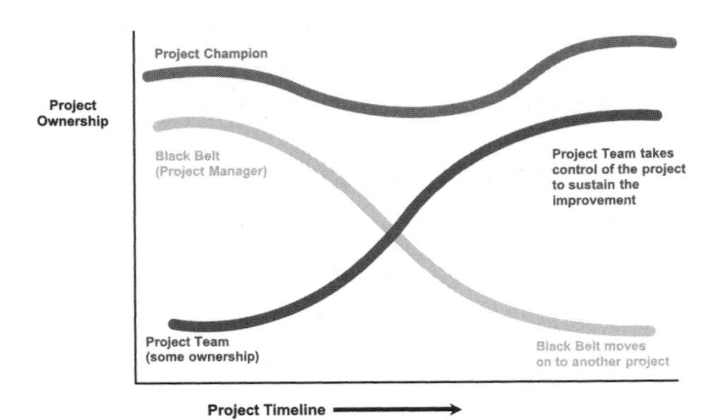

As a project moves toward completion, the project team increases project control while the project lead's role diminishes. This allows the team members to sustain the results of the project.

A project lead, with the help of the project champion, selects the team members based on the functional knowledge required for the project. Project leads usually consider the following when selecting team members:

- Six Sigma project experience
- Knowledge or experience with the customer
- Knowledge or experience with the current process
- Availability and projected dedication

If you're asked to be on a team, you should have some knowledge of how Six Sigma works. You might receive your training in a classroom setting or from your project leader throughout the life of the project. In addition, you will be expected to spend somewhere between 10 to 25 percent of your work week on the project, based on the needs of the project.

The Owner

At this point, we still haven't told you who truly owns the project. Who is responsible for achieving results? While many people think the project leader is accountable, it's actually the *process owner* who carries this load. In the vacuum cleaner example, while the store manager led the project, the vacuum cleaner department head actually had direct responsibility for vacuum cleaner sales. The department head was the one to ensure the changes would stick.

Sigma Sayings

The **process owner** is the person with direct responsibility for the production of an output.

So, if you own the output (vacuum cleaner sales), you have the most to gain from reducing the defect (lost sales). You also must accept and live with the change resulting from the project. By pushing ownership down to what is typically a mid-management position, you are combining a passion to succeed with strong functional knowledge. This is a major contributor to the power of Six Sigma.

While the process owner may not actively participate in the project, the project leader should regularly communicate every aspect of the project to the owner throughout the life of the project. Remember, the process owner must buy in to the ultimate changes a project team recommends. Without the support and assistance of the process owner during the implementation of the solution, the solution cannot succeed. The process owner is the sole person who will truly sustain the solution.

A Well-Oiled Machine

While strong corporate acceptance is one reason Six Sigma works, another can be found in the structured project management approach it utilizes. We will now discuss how Six Sigma really works.

Six Sigma solves business problems using the following approach:

- Identify the problem (or defect).
- Set a goal based on customer expectations.
- Find the process causing the defect.
- Validate the defect exists and to what extent.
- Determine the causes.
- Identify and test a sustainable solution to achieve your goal.

Every project begins with identifying a problem. However, with Six Sigma, a realistic goal for reducing the defect is established rather than just generically stating the problem will be fixed, which is common with traditional process improvement approaches. The goal is set by finding out *what* the customer wants. No guess work is needed and no surprises occur.

For instance, if customers define a faulty light bulb as one that lasts only two days and a manufacturing process is producing three faulty light bulbs in every run, the first step in Six Sigma will be to identify the problem—the production of faulty light bulbs. The second step is to set a goal for reducing the problem—for instance, producing one or fewer faulty light bulbs in every run.

Closely analyzing the defect will lead you directly to the process where the defects are being produced. In the faulty light bulb example, the production process might appear to be the problem. However, you might actually find that the process of distributing the light bulbs is producing the defect.

By formulating a team with a strong knowledge of the manufacturing and distribution processes, you can …

- Create a measurement system to validate the defect exists.
- Determine the process producing the defect.
- Identify the appropriate course of action to reduce or eliminate the defect.

By including the people who own the process in the solution definition, implementing change to correct the problem is a snap. However, the structured Six Sigma approach does more than just implement the change. Six Sigma uses rigor to test the changes prior to implementation and develops a plan to sustain the changes over time.

Included in this unique structured approach is a consistent method of communication. *Tollgates* or project reviews are used to ensure all critical people remain involved throughout the life of a project.

Sigma Sayings

Tollgates are scheduled meetings with project sponsors occurring at specific stages throughout the project to present clear project definitions, current findings, and the future direction of the project.

At this point, you are probably wondering how long it will take to complete a Six Sigma project. Because most businesses need results fast, Six Sigma relies on a relatively short timeframe to implement a solution. The Six Sigma methodology enforces narrowly scoped projects in an effort to produce results usually within three to six months.

Truth in the Numbers

All this sounds great, but what makes it stick? Why are so many companies willing to invest in a Six Sigma solution? How can your company be sure it will get enough bang for the buck? It's all in the data.

Six Sigma uses data to define the problem initially. It uses data to predict how various solutions will work. It uses data to select the appropriate solution. And, yes, Six Sigma even uses data to test the selected solution. By the time you put the solution in action, the data has spoken—so no one else needs to!

Let's explain how this works. Suppose you, a company officer, believe too much money is being spent on photocopies of learning materials. You then decide to collect historical data over a 12-month period to show the amount of money being spent. By comparing the data to the budget, the data tells you that you are over budget. The data has defined the problem.

By slicing and dicing the data, you can drill down to what is causing the problem. For instance, you might find most of the money is being spent on obsolete material or that too much of the material is sitting in inventory after being photocopied. You might even find through data analysis that most people are using alternate means for training, such as the Internet, which may not require the distribution of material.

After identifying possible solutions to the problem, data is collected and analyzed to determine which solution is the best. In most cases, the top solutions are tested and the testing results (more data) are reviewed to make the right choice. In the photocopies example, possible solutions to allow you to stay on budget might be:

- Elimination of obsolete material
- Reduction of inventory on preprinted material
- Alternatives to printed material

By continuing to measure resources spent on a monthly basis, you are using data to monitor your implemented solution. The data tells you if you are on target or quickly approaching going above target.

Problem → Validation → Cause → Solution → Sustainability

Communication
Data

Six Sigma uses a structured approach to problem-solving, incorporating communication and data in every step.

While Six Sigma's unique project structure ensures things get *done*, data makes sure things get done *the right way!*

The Least You Need to Know

- Six Sigma is the predominant choice for eliminating quality defects due to its use of a unique comprehensive tool set.
- Black belts lead Six Sigma projects full-time.
- Project champions should ensure corporate strategies are aligned with Six Sigma project selection.
- Process owners are primarily responsible for the defect reduction.
- Six Sigma uses a structured project management approach combined with data to reduce quality defects effectively.

The Technique

In This Chapter

- Six Sigma approaches to solving problems
- A close look at the DMAIC process

The most commonly used methodology is the DMAIC (duh-may-ick) process. It consists of five sequential steps: define, measure, analyze, improve, and control. The DMAIC process is applied primarily when problems occur within an *existing* process. This means you should use DMAIC when a measurable defect exists that is preventing, or causing a decrease in, customer satisfaction.

The five phases of DMAIC provide companies with a common framework to live by. This roadmap enables project leads, sponsors, and team members to speak the same language for solving problems and transition more easily from one business problem to the next. DMAIC …

- Enables project sponsors to ask the right questions and ensures the right tasks are accomplished during every phase.

- Sets a clear path for the project lead.
- Simplifies team member learning as team members participate on future projects.
- Increases the effectiveness of communication as terminology is shared and understood throughout the organization.

In this chapter, we dive head-long into the DMAIC approach and discuss how this technique, when used across the organization, provides consistency and continuity in project management for overall project success.

Define

The define phase is all about setting expectations. In this phase, a problem is turned into a specific goal that can be measured and solved in later phases. Specifically, during the define phase, a team will …

- Identify the defect.
- Determine the customer.
- Create a quantifiable goal including projected financial benefits for the project.
- Estimate the timeframe for project completion.
- Assemble resources.

Right Problems; Right Time

The define phase begins with identifying and narrowly defining the problem. Usually, data will exist that helps a project lead identify the problem. However, scoping the problem or breaking down the problem into smaller, more manageable pieces can be tough. For instance, if company sales dropped significantly from last year, a project lead might be asked to *fix sales*. To scope this for Six Sigma, they might ask, "What factors are causing the decreased sales?" Is it a lack of product, a lack of customer assistance, or due to a decrease in customer traffic? For this to be an effective Six Sigma project, more data would be needed to focus the project on the one area that is most related to causing the decrease in sales.

Process Pointers

Project leads have to be careful not to try to save the world by taking on a problem too large in scope. We call this *boiling the ocean*. If the project is too large, they might have difficulty finishing the project in a reasonable amount of time. Instead, the goal is to break down larger projects into smaller projects that can be worked on simultaneously or sequentially, producing results more quickly.

Another reason to scope projects carefully is that many businesses today believe that it is business-critical to complete projects in a three- to six-month timeframe or less. By keeping project cycle times short, businesses are better prepared to keep up with the changing demands of customers and board members.

The Customer

With Six Sigma, every problem (or defect) must be traced back to the process responsible for producing the problem. A problem of poor sales in Region A will point to looking at Region A's sales process. A problem of not efficiently scheduling employees to meet customer demands will point to looking at the scheduling process.

After finding the right process to address, the next step is to locate and understand the customer of the process. Understanding the customer is the most important step in the define phase. Often we jump into thinking we know what is important to the customer and create a solution that far exceeds the customer's expectations or, even worse, delivers a solution that doesn't meet the customer's expectations at all. The customer service world is ever evolving, so even if data exists to describe the customer's needs, the accuracy of this data must be validated.

Defect Alert

> When a customer's needs are not understood, the result of the project is often a solution that does not solve the original problem.

For example, a company that develops gloves for work on high-voltage power lines had the customer requirements of producing gloves without holes in bright orange. While performing a factory tour, one manager noted the large pile of rejected gloves. When asked about the large number of defects, the associate replied, "They are not the right color; the customer wants bright orange gloves." As a trial, the manager presented a sample of the rejected gloves to the customer, and asked, "Would you take these gloves?" The customer replied, "Do they have any holes?" The manager replied, "No," and the customer replied, "Yes, we will buy them." The associates in the manufacturing facility *assumed* they knew the brightness of the color of the gloves the customer wanted. Clearly, they were wrong.

Calculating the Sigma Value

After the customer's needs are identified and converted into process specifications, a baseline measure must be established. This is a measure that will be used throughout the process to gauge improvement. Examples of baseline measures are …

- The number of products in stock.
- The burn rate of in-stock items.
- The time required to restock a specific set of products.

After identifying the primary metric (the measurement you use to gauge success), the next step in the define phase is to convert this primary or baseline measure into a Process Sigma level. As we discussed in Chapter 1, a Process Sigma is a statistical term used to explain how much variation exists relative to customer expectations.

Calculating a Process Sigma begins with identifying how many defects per process output exist.

To meet customer expectations for the checkout process at a local grocery store, let's suppose the cashier is required to …

- Complete the checkout transaction in less than 55 seconds.
- Ring the items accurately.
- Be courteous.

Therefore, the checkout process contains 3 opportunities for a defect to occur. If 200 checkouts were observed and 10 total defects were identified, the Process Sigma would be calculated as follows:

1. Calculate the defects per opportunity:

   $10/(200 \times 3)$

2. Calculate the process yield:

   (1 – Defects per Opportunity) × 100 = 98.34

3. Look up Sigma in the Sigma process table (Appendix A):

   3.63*

**Based on short-term Sigma calculations.*

The resulting Process Sigma in this example is 3.63. Remember, 6.0 is near perfection. Many companies are happy to achieve Process Sigma somewhere between 3.0 and 4.0, depending on the customer impact and their expected quality level. However, if achieving a lower-quality Sigma level results in manufacturing faulty child safety seats, thereby causing life-threatening outcomes, the company's Sigma level goal will increase.

Customers Are King

With the baseline measure of the primary metric identified, a measurable goal for improvement can be set. This goal is based on expectations set by the customer, also known as a *customer specification.*

Sigma Sayings

Customer specification refers to a goal or requirement set by the customer based on the customer's needs.

If customers expect to find sales associates within three minutes when entering a store on a Saturday, a goal must be set to meet this customer expectation. This could result in a focus area of improving the customer-to-associate ratio, so associates can meet with customers within three minutes of entering the store.

At this point in the Six Sigma journey, we have used data to recognize a defect or improvement opportunity, identified the customer of the opportunity, turned the customer's input into process-delivery requirements (or goals), and identified the overall or high-level process producing the defect. The last steps before moving onto the measure phase are organizing the right project team and creating a timeline for expected project completion and associated financial benefit.

Measure

Let's go back to our original example where sales are dropping compared to previous years. Assume a project team found during the define phase that the opportunities for improvement were centered on key items, which were always out of stock. By using data and team input, the team should now be able to scope the project down to a more manageable level by reducing the out-of-stock conditions of the key items. In the measure phase, the team determines how widespread the problem is and collects enough data to explore possible causes of the problem. This is accomplished by …

- Validating existing data for accuracy.
- Determining whether the problem exists everywhere or just in certain situations.
- Identifying external factors or possible causes for the problem.

The first step in the measure phase is to check existing data for accuracy and fully understand where the data came from. For example, if a new system was implemented this year to track and report inventory levels, the project team might find a glitch in how the new system calculates inventory.

Defect Alert

Measuring the problem is an important step. If you don't, here's what can happen:

An engine manufacturing plant had a problem with pigeons in the duct work of the plant. The pigeons' waste was dispersed through the air ducts and vents causing people to become ill. The plant manager demanded the executives put a special noise in the factory that only pigeons could hear. He believed the noise would drive the pigeons away. Without data or testing, they agreed to put the noise in the factory. Today, the factory has *twice* the number of pigeons it had prior to implementing the manager's demanded solution.

The second step in the measure phase is for the project team to find out whether the problem, or improvement opportunity, is occurring everywhere in the business or just in certain instances or locations. For example, the team may dive deeper into the inventory numbers to determine whether certain weeks or quarters produced more out-of-stock conditions for high-selling items than other weeks or quarters. Likewise, they may want to collect inventory levels by product type, supplier, or distribution area to see whether the problem is related to any of these specific areas. This process of breaking down data is called *data stratification* and is used to determine where the problem exists.

Sigma Sayings

Data stratification refers to the process of dividing data into smaller groups based on factors identified by the project team. This could lead a project team to focus its work on a specific subgroup of the data population.

The third step in the measure phase is to collect data around other external factors that might be causing your problem. This collection effort starts with probably the simplest but most important tool, the process map. The process map requires the black belt or green belt to document the current process in detail. By studying the current process, a team is better prepared to identify all possible causes for the problem. Here's a list of a few factors that might cause out-of-stock conditions for the best-selling products:

- Manufacturing issues causing production slowdown
- Late shipping
- High turnover of inventory planners

With data stratification results and a list of potential causes, the team is ready to document a plan for collecting more detailed data. Where will the data come from? How will it be collected? Who will collect the data, and when will it be collected?

After a data collection plan is documented, the actual collection process must be tested. Testing the collection process can eliminate spending time and money collecting inaccurate data.

After the measure is completed, the team revisits the original baseline measure and Process Sigma calculated during the define phase. Sometimes these numbers must be updated based on new findings resulting from the data collection effort.

Analyze

Going back to our sales example, suppose we concluded that out-of-stock conditions are the main defect causing low sales. Also, suppose we found that the blue widgets had the largest decrease in sales, and we discovered that the in-stock position of the blue widgets over the past two years has been at 72 percent or a Sigma level of 0.58 (based on long-term Sigma calculations). Finally, assume we identified the reasons for the low in-stock position as …

- A decrease in product availability.
- Poor receiving practices.
- Inefficient order placement.

With the defect identified and the list of potential causes at hand, a DMAIC project team is ready for the analyze phase. This phase uses statistical analysis tools, which are described in Chapter 4, to narrow the many, various causes of the problem down to the vital few. For instance, we might find that all of the blue widgets were removed from the distribution list of stores in the northwest region. Or maybe a few of the key vendors producing blue widgets went out of business recently.

Even though we have identified possible causes of the defect, we do not yet have the *root cause*.

Sigma Sayings

Root cause refers to the most fundamental reason for a defect occurring repeatedly. When a root cause is removed, the defect is significantly reduced.

The root cause is found by looking for impacts on the customer and can be independent or related to other root causes. For example, with the collection of additional data, you might find that the cycle time required to produce blue widgets has recently doubled, causing severe back-orders. This would be an independent root cause—one clear reason for out-of-stocks occurring. On the other hand, the root cause of out-of-stocks of blue widgets could be due to the inefficient restocking of the product, combined with an error in the on-hand inventory system calculation. This would be an interaction of causes, resulting in dependent or related root causes.

The active participation of the project team during the analyze phase is the most critical of all the phases. Because these are the people closest to the broken process, their experiences and knowledge are critical to finding the root causes.

Improve

With the root cause of the defect known, the team is ready to make changes. During the improve phase, the team completes the following steps:

- Identify ways to eliminate the root cause.
- Test the top solution.
- Create an implementation plan.
- Implement the solution.

Suggestions are made to eliminate the root cause identified during the analyze phase by altering the process producing the root cause. The mission here is to change the process to show positive movement in the success metric. In our example, we must now change the way we restock blue widgets within the sell space of the store.

By identifying all possible solutions—big and small, expensive and cheap—the team is tasked with prioritizing the list of potential solutions, or modifying the root causes, in order to make the best selection. When prioritizing potential solutions, the team considers the following:

- Initial and on-going costs associated with the implementation of process modifications, such as annual maintenance agreements, annual compensation, infrastructure costs, and so on
- Hard- and soft-dollar benefits
- Level of effort required
- Potential problems or risks that might arise
- Customer satisfaction with the revised process

The next step in the improve phase is to test the top solutions. In some cases, the team tests the top two or three solutions to determine which solution shows the greatest impact. However, if the cost of testing multiple solutions is too high, the top priority solution will be tested and based on the results.

The team determines whether alternative solution testing is required.

Having identified our root cause as poor or ineffective restocking practices of blue widgets, the top three solutions might be prioritized as:

1. Retrain the night crew to move product more quickly.
2. Hire additional restocking associates who are trained just to handle blue widget restocking.
3. Develop a vendor-based inventory management process.

To test all three solutions would be quite costly. Instead, a team might test the first solution and determine whether the results showed a *statistically significant* improvement.

Sigma Sayings

A result that differs from the basis enough to suggest that the difference between the two is not by accident or coincidence is **statistically significant.**

For instance, if you retrained a sampling of the restocking crew and achieved a statistically significant reduction in out-of-stocks for blue widgets, it is probable you will continue to see the same level of improvement when the solution is fully implemented. However, training alone may not be the answer because training is an *event*, not a *process change*. Many times, positive results are achieved by simply training associates. However, this may be the result of the *Hawthorn Effect*, and might be misleading.

Sigma Sayings

The **Hawthorn Effect** refers to positive results seen from making a change to the environment of the associates. Based on the early quality studies of Hawthorn, improved results were seen in sewing factories by simply turning up the brightness of the factory lights. No significant change was made to the process, but the process improved. Over time, the quality level of the factory returned to its normal low-production levels.

To avoid the Hawthorn Effect of training, the team will want to select a process solution that changes the process, similar to that of hiring experts to handle the situation. This may be costly, but far less costly than losing sales of top items.

With the winning solution selected, the next step is to create a detailed implementation plan, including costs and benefits. The implementation plan may require additional input from employees outside the core project team. Having a solid plan results in fewer issues during implementation. It can also help identify critical resources and up-front costs that might need to be incorporated into the original costs and benefits identified. An implementation plan should include resources and timelines for …

- Development and implementation plans for any new tools or technology.
- Documentation of any new or changed procedures, job descriptions, and performance guidelines.
- The creation of training materials and communication.
- Training schedules, trainers, and trainees.

Executing the solution begins when the plan is approved by the project sponsor. In many cases, the plan should be reviewed and approved by other key members within the organization. For instance, if you are making reporting or job responsibility changes, a member of the human resources and legal groups within the company might review the plan to ensure all potential issues are addressed before implementing the solution.

Control

The solution is in place and the project lead is ready to move on to another project. Well, not so fast. While most improvement projects might stop here, the Six Sigma methodology brings in reinforcements to ensure the defect won't return. This last phase of DMAIC is called the control phase.

The focal point of the control phase is sustainability. Before the project lead can carve a notch on his belt and call the project complete, the following questions must be answered:

- How can we guarantee the improvement will continue?
- What happens if the defect returns?
- Who is responsible for maintaining the improvements over time and making modifications as the business changes?

During the control phase, the project team enhances the selected solution by developing methods to measure and track the live solution. With the creation of a control plan, resources are identified to ensure the on-going solution continues to produce the agreed-upon results.

The control plan also eliminates any guesswork when something goes wrong with the implemented solution. By documenting *contingency plans* within the control plan, the process owner is armed with alternatives in the event problems arise.

Just as businesses and customers continue to change, the implemented process must be flexible enough to change as well. Over time, the process owner is tasked with managing this change and adapting the new process to fit the changes appropriately.

Sigma Sayings

Contingency plans are detailed plans specifying alternative actions to take if something in the implemented solution goes wrong.

The last step in the control phase is to communicate the success of the project. Don't underestimate the importance of this. As mentioned earlier, the overall success of Six Sigma is in widespread adoption. The more people who understand and see the value of Six Sigma, the more readily they will accept and participate in future projects. By organizing and sharing the documentation and results achieved throughout the life of the project, other employees can learn the Six Sigma approach and understand the value it brings.

The Least You Need to Know

- DMAIC, a common project approach used in Six Sigma, includes the following phases: define, measure, analyze, improve, and control.
- The define phase requires a clear understanding of the problem the customer is facing.
- Collecting baseline data and identifying the many potential causes for failure occurs during the measure phase.

- Upon completing the analyze phase, you will have identified the key potential causes of your problem.
- The improve and control phases focus on sustainable process changes to eliminate the root causes of your problem.

The Tool Belt

In This Chapter

- Common tools for managing any type of project
- Tips to find exactly what your customer wants
- Approaches for identifying root causes
- How to select the best solution for your problem

In Chapter 3, we discussed the DMAIC steps (define, measure, analyze, improve, and control) used to complete a Six Sigma project. However, following these steps alone will not solve your business problem. Only when the steps are used in combination with other key tools can you begin to see results.

Interestingly, the tools used in Six Sigma are not unique to Six Sigma. In other words, the Six Sigma tools were not created as a result of discovering the Six Sigma methodology. In fact, the tools used in Six Sigma are tools that have been around for many years. Some of the tools have been used in other process improvement and quality improvement methodologies, some have been used in science and statistical research, and others have been used by businesses as part of basic project planning and execution.

A Six Sigma project lead, usually with the help of a master black belt, determines which tools are appropriate for a given project. A black belt, for example, usually works on more sophisticated problems and, therefore, may utilize more tools than a green belt, who spends less time on less complex projects. The key to successful and timely completion of Six Sigma projects is understanding all available tools and using those that make the most sense for solving the problem.

Project Management 101

Successfully completing Six Sigma projects requires strong project organization beginning in the define phase. Most projects require upward, downward, and sideways communication. This means the project lead is constantly trying to help the executive sponsor, his peers, and the project team members understand the direction, goals, timeline, and commitments of the project.

Project Charter

Creating a project charter at the start of a project ensures everyone is on the same page. A charter is a brief document that defines the following:

- Project resources
- Problem statement and current Sigma level
- Scope
- Goals and projected Sigma level
- Financial benefits
- Project schedule, including key milestones

Charters should not be more than one page. Remember, this tool is designed to share critical information about a project. People need to read and understand the charter! Most importantly, we encourage project leads to update constantly. The charter is the main communication tool throughout the life of the project, so it's important to keep it current as the project proceeds.

A sample template of a project charter may include the following:

> During the time frame of *(MM/YY)* to *(MM/YY)*, the *(measure of process)* of the *(title of the process)* process was *(enter value)*. Compared to the customer specifications of *(enter specification limits)*, the process is performing at a Sigma level of *(enter Sigma level)*. The focus of this project is to reduce the defects of this process by *(enter goal)*, in a time frame of *(enter project duration)*, to provide a company benefit of *(enter benefit)*.

Work Plan

A work plan is a detailed schedule of the actions the team will perform on the project, including an estimated completion date for each action. Documenting tasks in a work plan can help the team more accurately forecast the ultimate completion date of the project.

Work plans also communicate to a team which tasks are dependent on other tasks. A common work plan style used in many Six Sigma projects is the Gantt chart style, displayed in the following figure.

When creating a work plan, the team leader must know he cannot complete everything alone. Defining accountability for task completion is critical for a project manager to meet his deadlines. By identifying the responsible team member's name directly on the work plan next to each task, the team lead is encouraging task ownership.

Tollgates

While detailed documentation provides great team communication, face-to-face project reviews are critical to …

- Solicit feedback.
- Gain funding.
- Communicate findings.
- Update project direction.

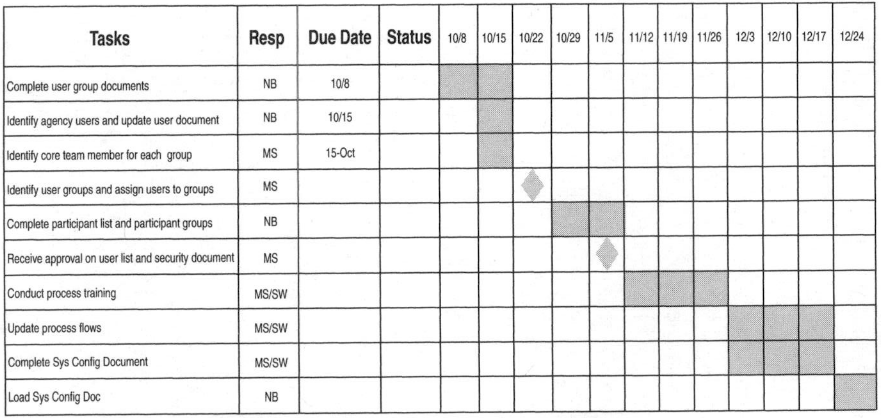

Tasks	Resp	Due Date	Status	10/8	10/15	10/22	10/29	11/5	11/12	11/19	11/26	12/3	12/10	12/17	12/24
Complete user group documents	NB	10/8													
Identify agency users and update user document	NB	10/15													
Identify core team member for each group	MS	15-Oct													
Identify user groups and assign users to groups	MS														
Complete participant list and participant groups	NB														
Receive approval on user list and security document	MS														
Conduct process training	MS/SW														
Update process flows	MS/SW														
Complete Sys Config Document	MS/SW														
Load Sys Config Doc	NB														

A Gantt chart–style work plan will display start and end dates for tasks along with task dependencies and key milestones.

This Six Sigma approach of regular project reviews is called a tollgate. Tollgates are used to track and measure the progress of a project.

The most successful Six Sigma projects have tollgates that are attended by the project lead, mentor, or master black belt; the project champion; and the area finance person. Other master black belts are encouraged to attend to proliferate project knowledge and ultimately eliminate duplicate project efforts.

The Almighty Customer

Many tools exist to help companies define who their customers are and find out what these customers want. We take a look at some of these helpful tools in the following sections.

SIPOC

A *SIPOC (Supplier, Inputs, Process, Output, Customer) diagram* is a tool used to help identify the customer. Starting with the area believed to be producing the problem—the process—the team lead works the SIPOC outward to identify the process inputs and the process outputs. Next, the suppliers of the inputs are identified along with the customers (or recipients) of the process output. In addition to helping determine the most critical aspect of a project—the customer—a SIPOC diagram is helpful in illustrating the scope of any project.

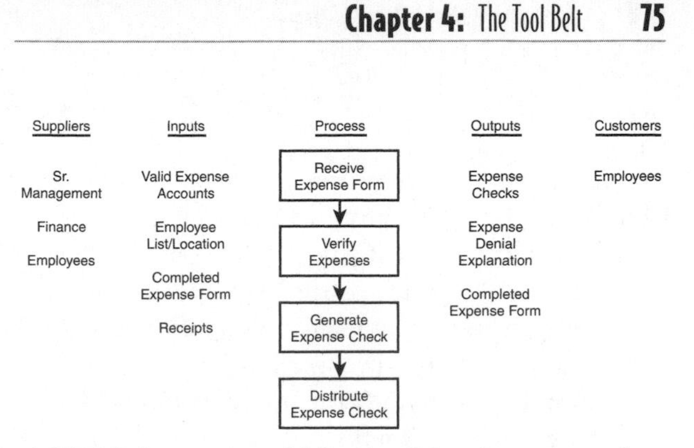

A SIPOC diagram is useful for identifying the customer of a process.

Voice of the Customer

If you planned a party for your daughter, you probably collected information to determine what your customers (your daughter and her friends) wanted. You might have interviewed your daughter and a few of her friends to find out what they liked about other parties, researched age-appropriate parties on the Internet, or attended parties and observed reactions. These different methods of data gathering all play a part in defining the *voice of the customer* or VOC.

VOC data is used to determine what customers want and, sometimes, what they don't want. Some VOC data can be readily available in the form of complaints and suggestions, but often this requires companies to actively collect this information through the use of surveys, interviews, and research.

CTQ

Knowing what the customer wants is not enough. The VOC must be converted into *Critical to Quality Characteristics* (*CTQs*). These characteristics are then used to create process specification limits. Furthermore, a project team has to differentiate between the nice-to-have's and the must-have's. In addition, they search for the point at which the company achieves diminishing returns. This means the company is giving the customer *more* than they need. For example, if you enjoy dining in restaurants that are efficient, have great food, an enjoyable atmosphere, and good prices, these are the items the restaurant must provide to please you as a customer. If the restaurant owner insists on giving away free desserts, something the customer does not expect, he may delight his customers but exceed his expenses and unnecessarily reduce his profits.

CTQs are the specific things that are critical to quality in the customers' minds. Without the CTQs, customers will not be satisfied with a company's product or service due to the fact that CTQs drive specification limits. By translating VOC data into CTQs, and CTQs into specification limits, a clear metric or goal can be defined.

The Measuring Cup

Measurements are used across all aspects of Six Sigma including …

- Creating a baseline.
- Measuring varying causes.
- Quantifying potential solutions.

Because of the wide use of measurements, you should not be surprised to discover that many tools are available to accurately define and execute measurements of a process, as well as display measurement results for analysis.

Measurement System Analysis

All data collection efforts should begin with a Measurement System Analysis (MSA). An MSA determines whether the variation found in the measurements is due to the quality defect or the measurement system. Measurement variation can result from …

- Inconsistencies among different people performing the same measure with the same measuring tool, also known as *operator-to-operator variation.*
- Inconsistencies resulting each time the same person measures the same thing using the same measuring tool, also known as *within-operator variation.*

Performing an MSA requires the creation of a detailed *measurement plan*.

Sigma Sayings

A **measurement plan** refers to a document describing the specific measuring tool, including instructions on how the tool will be used, and a list of who will use the tool.

A measurement plan for measuring customer wait times might describe the use of a stop watch in addition to providing clear definitions of when the customer's wait time starts and when it ends. The execution of the MSA would consist of three to five stop watch users measuring the same five customers who complete the wait-in-line process. The MSA would measure the accuracy between the measurers' variation. The only way to truly measure each operator's variation would be to have the same operator measure the same process experience several times. For example, if a store had tapes of 10 customer wait-in-line experiences, and the operator, or measurer, watched the tapes and performed the measurement process for each customer on the tape, and then repeated the tape-watching process four to five times, we could measure the *repeatability* or *within variation*, of the operator. A Gauge R&R (repeatability and reproducibility) test can help assess the results of your measurement system analysis.

Control Charts

So what do we do with all the data after we finish measuring the process? First, we want to look for clues in the data to help us identify when and where the variation is occurring. With the use of control charts, the team can identify patterns in the data to help determine what type of variation exists and how relevant the variation is.

A *control chart* provides a view of the data over time. If customer wait times are being measured for a call center, we might measure the wait times throughout the day to determine whether call times are longer in the morning or afternoon.

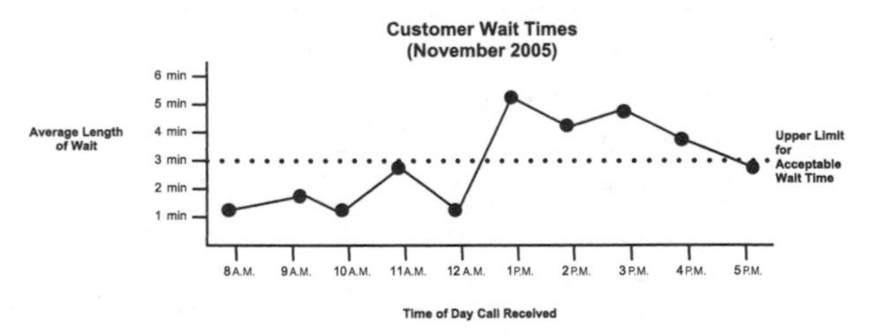

A control chart is used to identify patterns over time.

Another reason for using a control chart is to separate *special cause* from *common cause* variation. Special cause variation occurs in a process when something out of the ordinary occurs at a specific point in time. A reason for this odd occurrence can usually be explained. For instance, suppose you were tracking component placement cycle time for a manufacturing process and found an incredibly low cycle time one day. If, through further investigation, you found the reason to be due to a fire drill lasting two hours that day, this would be defined as a special cause. Common cause variation, on the other hand, occurs throughout the process. While eliminating special causes will provide improvements to the overall process, Six Sigma focuses on reducing the common cause variation by implementing permanent changes to the process.

Frequency Plot

Another method for reviewing data is a *frequency plot*. A frequency plot shows you how often a particular event occurs. In our call center example, how often are calls with over three minutes wait times occurring throughout the day?

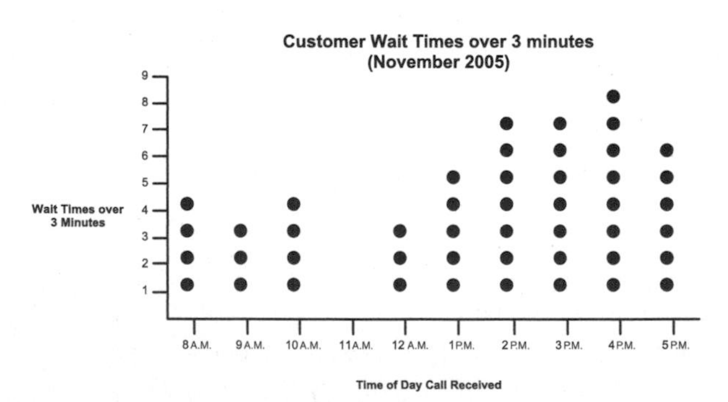

A frequency plot shows how often an event occurs.

Frequency plots can also help determine where special cause variation versus common cause variation is occurring. Analyzing the shape of the plot or the distribution of the data points suggests the level of stability inherent in the process.

Pareto Charts

Similar to a frequency plot, a *pareto chart* identifies how often an event occurs within a specific category. This type of chart is often used to narrow the scope of a project by selecting the category where the problem occurs most often.

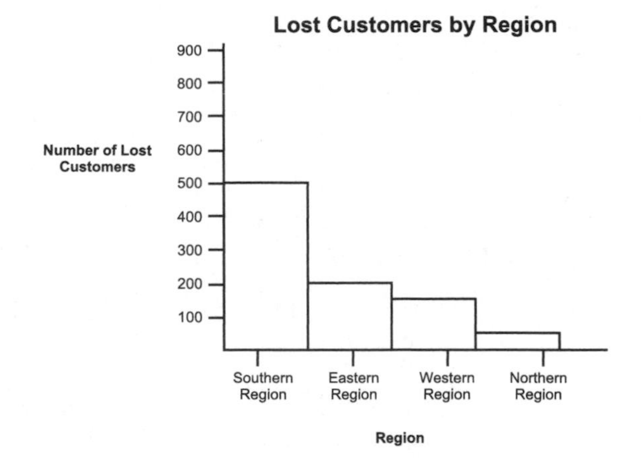

A pareto chart shows how often an event occurs across various categories.

Pareto charts can be used to compare data across categories such as …

- Regions.
- Manufacturing plants.
- Reason codes.
- Product types.

Slicing and Dicing

Luckily, Six Sigma also pulls together many tools used to determine *why* a problem is occurring. These are referred to as the *causal factors* (or the Xs) for the problem. The problem (Y) is then defined as a result of one or more Xs. You might also see this in the form of a mathematical equation: Y=f(x). Or simply, Y is a function of X.

Sigma Sayings

The **Six Sigma equation,** Y=f(X), refers to a problem or process output, which is defined as the result or cause of one or more Xs or inputs. Eliminating or improving the Xs reduces or eliminates the problem. Controlling the Xs provides a greater forecast or predictability of the output Y, enabling a proactive process control methodology as opposed to reactive.

For example, if you are trying to reduce the number of meals sent back to the kitchen in a restaurant (Y), you might identify potential causes (Xs) as follows:

1. The waiter wrote down the wrong order.
2. The kitchen prepared the wrong order.
3. The customer didn't like the order.

Orders sent back to the kitchen are a function of the wrong order written, the wrong order prepared, and the wrong order ordered. If any one of these causal factors is reduced, the number of defects will be reduced.

Brainstorming and Affinity Diagramming

Brainstorming is a technique used most commonly in Six Sigma for identifying the possible causes of a problem. Brainstorming consists of bringing people together to generate ideas in an open, unstructured environment. A brainstorming session usually includes a facilitator whose primary responsibility is to keep the group focused, encourage participation, and document the findings.

Often, the ideas resulting from a brainstorming session are categorized and shared as an affinity diagram. The affinity diagram can help a team understand the key ideas from the session and identify the next steps to take.

ALERT

Defect Alert

It's important to make people comfortable during a brainstorming session. This promotes creativity and ensures key points are discussed. Facilitators should avoid mixing bosses with direct reports, criticizing ideas, and not planning enough time for the session.

Whether searching for methods to measure a problem, looking for causes of the problem, or searching for fixes, brainstorming can be a valuable way to share ideas.

The 5 Whys

As we discussed earlier, Six Sigma focuses on getting to and eliminating the root cause of a problem. By using the 5 Whys approach, a team can dive deep into the heart of the problem.

The 5 Whys takes each cause individually and asks why the cause is occurring. Each time an answer (a deeper cause) is provided, a facilitator will ask "Why?" and continue down this path until the root cause is found.

For example:

> The customer is dissatisfied. Why(1)? They were not able to buy the product they wanted. Why(2)? We were out of stock. Why(3)?

The product was not delivered to the store. Why(4)? No order was placed. Why(5)? The ordering system was down. Why(6)? And so on.

Cause and Effect

Multiple approaches exist for identifying root causes. Like the 5-Whys tool, cause-and-effect diagrams and tree diagrams start with the process problem and continue to drill down to the reasons why the problem is occurring. These two tools are also helpful in understanding relationships between causes and can help analyze multiple causes simultaneously.

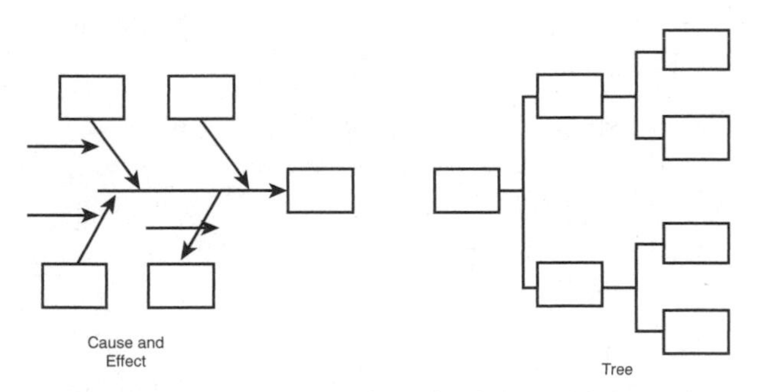

Cause-and-effect and tree diagrams are visual tools used to display relationships between variables.

Similarly, a Failure Mode and Effect Analysis (FMEA) is used to analyze all potential *ways* a process might fail as well as potential *reasons* why the process might fail. For instance, if you have identified a new process and want to prevent failure from occurring, an FMEA should be developed to address potential problems. An FMEA rates the potential failures based on:

- Severity—How bad is this failure?
- Frequency of occurrence—How likely is the failure to happen?
- Failure detection options—Do options exist to detect failures?

By rating the potential failures or risks for a process, a team can determine which potential failures should be addressed and which are less important. This calculation, based on severity, risk, and detection, is known as a Risk Priority Number (RPN). A higher RPN usually means you should focus on that segment of the process.

Project teams often use more than one tool for identifying and displaying causal relationships. Using a combination guides them down the right path to solving the problem.

Fine Tuning

These next sets of tools help determine which causes, if eliminated or modified, will improve a process. In some cases, relationships exist *between* causes. By removing only one of the related causes, you could create unexpected results.

Scatter Plots

Scatter plots can show relationships between two factors. The two factors might be two causes or the relationship between a cause and effect. The pattern of the scatter plot helps you determine whether a positive relationship, negative relationship, or no relationship exists. For instance, a positive relationship between a carpet installer's experience and his average hourly rate might suggest that, as the installer's experience goes up, his average hourly rate might also increase. If you are plotting the relationship between warm temperatures and the sales of winter clothes, you will likely find a negative relationship. As the temperature rises, the sales of winter clothes usually decrease.

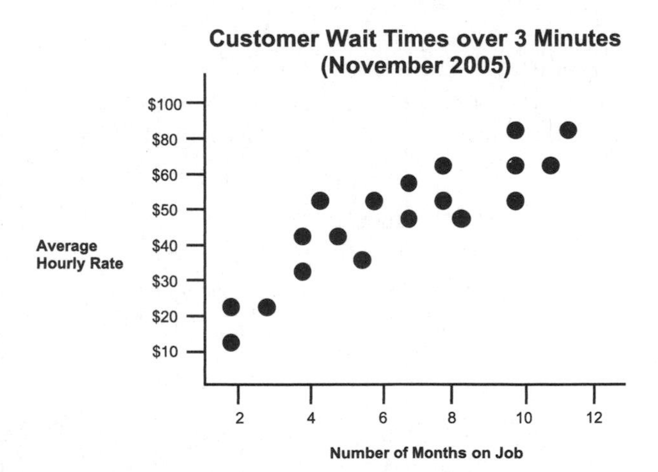

Scatter plots display relationships between factors.

Understanding relationships between factors can be helpful when developing solutions. If a solution is identified that will change the value of Factor 1, and Factor 1 is shown to have a relationship to Factor 2, the team may change its course of action to prevent changes from occurring to Factor 2.

Design of Experiment

A Design of Experiment (DOE) can combine multiple factors and test the effects of these factors on a process. For instance, if the team is unable to isolate one causal factor, it may be because the defect is a result of an interaction of two or more factors. For example, you may have three factors that you believe are related to the cause of the defect. Independently, the data shows that none of the three factors causes the defect. However, through a DOE test, you may find the causes have a significant impact on the process defect when the right combination of the three factors is determined.

To understand this more clearly, let's take a closer look. If we believe that store type, store location, and employee experience are critical factors of our process output, but none show a significant improvement independently, a DOE may be used to determine whether an interaction of these factors has a significant impact on the process output.

Benchmarking

Sometimes, even though the team has found the factor causing the problem by using statistical analysis, it may not know the best way to eliminate the problem. Benchmarking, or asking other companies how they operate, can provide ideas on the best way to attack problems.

ALERT

Defect Alert

Before your team talks with other companies, create a common list of questions to be sure the right information is gathered during each visit or call. You may also want to seek legal assistance with a nondisclosure agreement.

Often, noncompeting companies will share best practices, organizational alignments, and recommended procedures. In addition, employees within your own organization might offer valuable insights into processes they utilized while at previous companies.

Pugh Matrix

A Pugh Matrix is another tool to assist teams in finding the best solution for their problem. When multiple solutions exist for eliminating root causes, charting each solution based on the ability to address the CTQs, along with ease of implementation and financial return, can help the team make the right choice.

For instance, if your team identified two options as addressing the customer CTQs, a Pugh Matrix could be used to show that Option 2 is the better choice because of the longer, more expensive implementation required for Option 1.

Process Maps

As we discussed with SIPOC diagrams, whether participating in a Six Sigma project or just looking for a better way to do a job, a process map is the answer. By defining the work steps, owners, inputs, and outputs of a process, a process map can be used early in the measure phase to understand the current process, and then again in the improve phase to document how the proposed solution, or new process, will work.

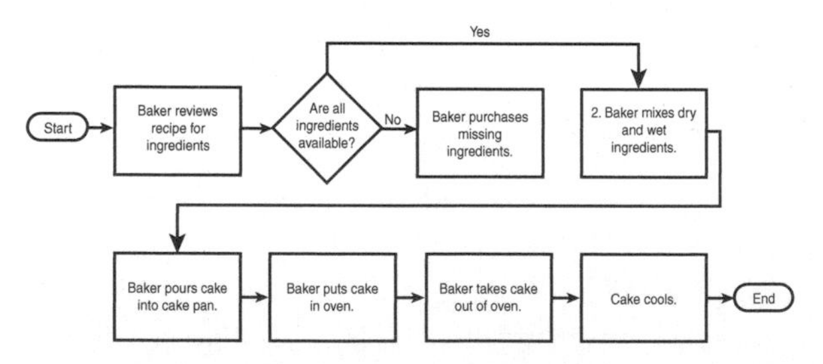

This process map displays the steps to bake a cake.

Often, the results of mapping an existing process quickly display redundant or duplicative tasks. Sometimes, even non–value-added tasks are identified by displaying outputs for each process step.

A to-be process map aimed at defining an improved process provides insight into roles and responsibilities and insures all steps have been considered. To-be process maps are great reference materials for use in creating training materials, procedure documents, and job descriptions.

A Combo

When starting a project, past experience has shown the use of three very common tools. The first tool used is the process map—detailing the process from start to finish. On the process map, you identify the output (Y) and the inputs to each step. The second tool used is a cause-and-effect diagram, which is used to organize the causes of process problems (Xs) relative to the process (Y). Using team member input, the top two or three Xs are identified on the cause-and-effect diagram. Then using the process map, you identify the block in the process where the significant Xs reside. At this point, you have focused your efforts on a single step within the process map. The third tool used is the FMEA, which can be performed at this point to identify all possible reasons (sub Xs) for why that step of the process might fail. After you have reached this point, more data is needed and further tests should be run to statistically prove that you have found the Xs that cause you to produce unsatisfactory products or services for the customer.

Try It! You'll Like It

Any time changes are made within an organization, it is a good idea to test the changes in a real-world setting before going live with the new process.

Pilots

A pilot is a test performed on a small scale, and it provides a great opportunity to learn what works within a subset of the entire population. The results of the pilot are used to determine how the solution might work on a larger scale. While companies may have to invest money in this test initially, they will likely save money in the long run by finding issues otherwise not considered that could impact the larger rollout.

Examples of problems uncovered during a pilot include …

- A problem in the process design.
- An issue with how training is administered.
- Difficulties with the method selected for implementation.
- Different results than expected against the defect.
- No measurement or tracking system for process accountability.

Remember, humans make mistakes. The pilot is the last opportunity to find things that may not have been considered throughout the life of the project.

Hypothesis Testing

So, how does the team know whether the pilot was truly successful? If no apparent problems are experienced, does that mean the team is ready to roll out the solution? Not yet. The team must be sure the results from the pilot show a *statistical improvement* over the original process. Otherwise, they might spend a lot of money implementing something that isn't that much better than what existed before.

Sigma Sayings

Statistical improvement refers to an improvement proven to be real with the use of mathematical tools. Data shows that the improvement was not a result of random variation.

Hypothesis testing tools, such as ANOVA, t-test, Chi-Square, and proportion tests, can all be used to determine if a true difference exists between two groups. In this case, the team is comparing the pilot group to the original baseline results.

Because hypothesis tests can be used to compare two groups, these tools can also be used during the analyze phase to determine whether an existing group performs better than another existing group. For example, phone center operators in the Northern region may be able to handle calls more quickly than those in the Southern region. To validate this hypothesis, a test is performed to prove whether a statistical difference in the results between the Northern region and Southern region really exists.

Stakeholder Analysis

The last tool we want to discuss is actually one of the first tools used in the DMAIC process: the stakeholder analysis. The stakeholder analysis is a listing of all key stakeholders for a project along with the type of communication required. Stakeholders are people who may touch the current or future process in any way, shape, or form. By continually updating this list and documenting the type of relationship each person has to the project, effective communication can be provided to the right people at the right time.

We can't stress enough how important communication is throughout all phases of the project. For instance, if the team gets down to selecting a pilot group, and the key leaders of the group have not been involved or are unaware of the project, the pilot might be stalled or stopped based on resistance from this group. Remember, the best form of communication targeted at the wrong people results in useless communication. A project team must know who to keep informed and the type of detail to provide.

Defect Alert

To ensure accurate information is provided to the right people at the right time, categorizing key stakeholders into groups is the best method to use. This allows team leaders to create varied forms of communication based on the group type. For instance, executive-level stakeholders might only want an overview and, therefore, demand less detail than a group of master black belts, who generally prefer to know every detail.

The Least You Need to Know

- Work plans are useful for keeping your project team on track and productive.
- Using charts to display and analyze your data helps you find patterns that can lead to solutions.
- A process map is an important tool for understanding the steps and owners of a process.
- A pilot is your last chance to effectively test your proposed solution prior to implementing it.

Chapter 

Belts That Fit

In This Chapter

- How to select belts for your organization
- Certification programs for belts
- Tips on administering effective training
- Using rewards and communication to spread adoption

People play a huge role in the success of Six Sigma and improving process quality. They do everything from managing projects, participating on teams, and encouraging project creation to supporting changes brought on by project results. Finding the right people is only the start. Knowing how to keep people involved in Six Sigma while you educate new people is vital. Remember, the primary goal for an organization implementing Six Sigma is to spread the practice across as many employees as possible.

In this chapter, we help you find black belts, green belts, and other lower belts—including brown, white, or orange—from inside or outside your organization. We do this by identifying the required skills that generate success. We give you insight on how you can use training programs to develop associates and spread Six Sigma practices throughout your organization. Finally, we talk about reward and certification programs to encourage participation and keep people in the program.

Selecting the Players

Finding the right people to lead projects is critical to implementing and maintaining a successful Six Sigma program. Understanding the skills required to lead Six Sigma projects helps you understand how project leads are selected.

What to Look For

Interestingly, the skills required to lead a project are the same skills that separate leaders from nonleaders. It's not a surprise that many organizations view these "belt" roles as great opportunities to breed leaders. The leadership qualities most companies look for are …

- Effective listening.
- Communication of ideas across various groups.
- Strong analytical skills.
- Commitment to make things better.
- Commitment to the organization.

Black belt project leads are usually selected because they have demonstrated leadership capabilities in the past, or they have the potential to be a leader in the future. In some cases, they have demonstrated leadership capabilities as Six Sigma project leads. However, they also might have managed other improvement projects successfully. These are typically people with a proven track record for effectively managing large-scale projects. They have the know-how to lead facilitated sessions, manage teams, and implement change. In addition, they understand all aspects of managing a business unit.

Green belt selection often focuses less on project leadership experience and more on the display of functional leadership combined with a proven ability to learn. Providing Six Sigma training and experience is a common approach to growing tomorrow's leaders.

Employees who are engaged in the lower-level belt programs are individuals who have the ability to make significant contributions to the Six Sigma team and lead a small-scale project.

The Search

So how do organizations find these people? Some organizations rely on executives to recommend leaders within their areas to fill these roles. Many companies establish specific criteria that each candidate must meet before becoming a belt. The criteria might include ...

- Specific scores from personality and analytic tests.
- Structured interview results.
- Work performance history.
- Executive recommendations.

For companies searching outside the organization to fill belt positions, many recruiting firms are available to assist in finding quality people. Companies might use the recruiting firm option to fill the master black belt positions, and then use this role as the focal point to research and find resources to fill the black belt roles. The new master black belt would work closely with the functional leaders to identify those who have a balance of Six Sigma knowledge combined with internal functional knowledge.

Measure, Again

Luckily, success in selecting the right green belt or black belt can be measured. As we discussed previously, almost every output can be traced back to a process. A hired belt is the direct output of a selection process. By identifying Critical to Quality Characteristics (CTQs) of a black belt at the time of the Six Sigma program formation, companies can monitor progress against these CTQs and determine when improvements are needed.

Reviewing project results is one way a company can determine whether the selection process is acceptable. Other metrics such as turnover, project-completion cycle times, financial savings, and Sigma-level increases can all be used to evaluate the success of the selection process.

Process Pointers

When companies identify and track metrics against predefined goals for belts, they have better success in continually improving their belt-selection processes.

However, in addition to the metrics defined above, selection success also should be evaluated based on the belt's continued use of Six Sigma throughout his employment within your company. Because most belt positions are temporary (two years on average), the true test is finding candidates who will be committed to Six Sigma as they reach other positions throughout their career. If the candidate continues to use the Six Sigma way of thinking long after his belt position is over, the company has made a good decision.

On-going use of Six Sigma includes more than just using the tools and methods. It also requires educating and developing others on Six Sigma. As true Six Sigma leaders progress in their roles, they carry the expectations that all their employees use

Six Sigma techniques. Ex-belts have an on-going role in the company to promote and spread the Six Sigma methodology.

ALERT

Defect Alert

Because black belt certification can vary from company to company, when hiring black belts from the outside, interviewers should ensure detailed qualifications are identified. Making assumptions related to the certification can result in poor hiring practices and poor candidate selection.

Certification

Currently, an informal certification process for belts exists. We call it *informal* because there is no governing board for Six Sigma similar to what exists for certified public accountants, lawyers, doctors, and so on. Still, most companies use a comparable standard for certifying belts.

Black belt certification usually requires mandatory attendance at all Six Sigma training classes. These classes can last anywhere from four to six weeks and involve project management training, methodology, in-depth data analysis, and statistics. Often, training on selected software tools used in charting and analyzing data is included. In some cases, tests are administered within the training classes to ensure the understanding of key concepts and that certification can be achieved.

In addition to training, the successful completion of projects is typically a requirement for certification. Successful project completion is usually defined as the completion of all associated tollgates. However, just finishing the project is not enough. A project resulting in a Sigma-level increase based on a predefined company metric is usually required. Some companies require certain financial gains to be achieved as well. The number of projects to complete varies across companies, but most companies require the completion of two to three projects before certification can be achieved.

Some companies also require a time commitment to the Six Sigma program. The time frames companies use to maximize the output from their black belts ranges from 12 to 24 months. This timeframe requirement assures the company that the individual black belts have the time to complete enough projects to show a significant return on the training investment.

Finally, most companies have a certification exam black belts must pass when the project requirement is met. The exam is usually in the form of a written test containing a combination of terminology and project process questions along with real application of the tools. Some companies create tests internally while other companies purchase exams from Six Sigma training and consulting organizations. A good test is designed to identify whether the black belt can apply his learned knowledge, not just recite the information in the text.

Green belt certification requirements are even more varied than black belt certification requirements. In fact, some companies do not have a certification process for this level. Instead, upon completion of green belt training, these folks are referred to as green belts. Still, some companies differentiate between green belts and *certified* green belts. The difference is often the number of projects completed successfully and, in some cases, the passing of a green belt exam.

The training requirement for a green belt is often about two weeks and focuses primarily on project management tools and Six Sigma concepts.

Lower-belt certifications are often based on class attendance. Brown, white, and even orange belts usually attend classes on change management that are sprinkled with define and measure concepts. These lower-level belts usually participate as team members, and thus the overview of the define and measure phases during their belt training helps them to better participate in team events, such as brainstorming and solution selection.

Most companies require master black belts to meet four major requirements prior to achieving certification:

- Teach the Six Sigma material administered by the company.

- Mentor other belts and demonstrate this proficiency under the guidance of an existing master black belt.
- Lead a super project.
- Attend advance learning classes.

First, certified master black belts usually must manage and administer a certain number of classes. These can be a combination of various Six Sigma classes, including green belt, black belt, and executive overview classes. Often, a certified master black belt is present in the initial classes to evaluate the training technique used in the class.

Because mentoring other belts is a major responsibility for a master black belt, a certification requirement is usually tied to the quality and quantity of the belts mentored. This usually includes a minimum of five belts and includes mentoring each belt throughout the life of each project. Again, a certified master black belt must be present during the mentoring sessions.

Although master black belts were black belts in the past, a major requirement to become a certified master black belt is the completion of a large-scale or super project. The results of this project should ultimately change the way a segment of your company does business. Usually, this project contains many related Six Sigma projects underneath and has a major impact on company results.

Process Pointers

As the newly trained black belts begin to apply their knowledge to their projects, they depend on the knowledge and experience of a master black belt. If the project mentor is a master black belt-in-training or a master black belt who is attaining a certification, they may not be capable of mentoring black belts by themselves. Therefore, it is critical to shadow all master black belts-in-training during all their mentoring sessions.

Lastly, many companies insist on the completion of additional training classes to achieve master black belt certification. The class requirements, again, vary by the company but might include …

- Statistical software classes.
- Leadership essentials.
- Business acumen.

While certification does not formally exist at an executive level, many companies implement a project scorecard approach to increasing executive-level involvement in Six Sigma. Used in conjunction with annual performance evaluations, a scorecard shows the number of successful projects initiated and completed. Rewards based on scorecard results can also have a large impact on eliminating project roadblocks as well as increase the number of successfully completed projects! The scorecard is the basis of holding executives accountable for Six Sigma project completions.

Spreading the Word

Creating a training program specific to the individual company's needs will increase acceptance and encourage Six Sigma practice throughout an organization. The more employees know, the more they will accept change when Six Sigma hits their area. Most importantly, they are more likely to use the tools to make improvements within their own areas.

Training CTQs

A large percentage of associates in your organization will eventually receive some type of Six Sigma training or overview. A training goal, usually set by an executive in your organization, identifies who should be trained, what type of training they should receive, and in what timeframe the training should occur.

Training goals are usually established by an organization early in a Six Sigma adoption. While training the entire organization's population would be great, most organizations are left to balance the training expense with the number of people to train. Training goals take into account the feasible number of expected completed projects annually and the associated benefits of each project. Large companies often establish a training department focused specifically on Six Sigma learning. This group partners with a Six Sigma operational group to establish curriculum requirements, manage and track training goals, and execute training. The size of the training department varies based on the training goals identified.

Smaller companies might purchase training services from outside organizations. These organizations can train employees on-site, or companies can choose to send their employees to off-site classes attended by multiple organizations, known as open enrollment learning.

Defect Alert

Companies using outside training services often risk purchasing materials that exclude functional examples related to the specific industry of the organization.

Training Execution

The top-down approach to training is the most effective method to rolling out a new Six Sigma training program. Because the executive group is sponsoring projects, teaching this group first makes perfect sense. Executives and sponsors should understand the fundamentals of Six Sigma to be effective in their roles. This includes communicating the value of Six Sigma with real-life examples, discussing the project approach, identifying how to define projects, and providing an overview of the primary tools available to project teams. Most importantly, as project sponsors, the executive group should be trained on what questions to ask and what to expect from project leads. Finally, a lesson on how to define project goals and benefits is also important.

The core of a company's training program is centered around the training of project leads or belts. As mentioned previously, black belt and green belt training focuses on project management skills combined with in-depth training on Six Sigma tools and methodology. Of course, a black belt training program includes more statistical tools and methods of analysis than a green belt training program. In addition, black belts are trained on statistical software that can be used to display and analyze data quickly. Both the green belt and black belt training curriculums include hands-on problem-solving techniques and include role-playing opportunities. Process owner training is also different from the aforementioned training programs. Process owner training focuses on key tools to help process owners continue to improve the processes they own. Incorporated in this training is an overview of the Six Sigma methodology with an emphasis on everyday tools process owners can use.

Process Pointers

When a company incorporates its own examples of Six Sigma success into its training programs, it energizes associates to increase their Six Sigma knowledge.

Other associates might receive training in a variety of ways. This training may be labeled as brown, white, or some other lower-level color of belt. The learning at this level of belt could be reinforced by having the candidate participate on a project team. Lower-belt training is usually offered to large audiences so knowledge is transferred to the masses. Other learning, which is expected to occur on all Six Sigma projects, is performed by the project lead because they provide some training on key Six Sigma concepts. These associates (or project team members) also get first-hand experience using the methodology as they participate in every phase of the project.

Process Pointers

Overview classes are short in length to encourage attendance by a large number of associates and provide a taste of Six Sigma. Associates usually sign up for more detailed classes following an overview class.

Six Sigma overview classes also can be administered to reach associates who may not have worked on a team. Six Sigma overview class topics include …

- Major Six Sigma concepts.
- DMAIC (define, measure, analyze, improve, and control) phase objectives.
- Examples of Six Sigma successes throughout the organization.

À la Carte

Executing training in small chunks is a good way to encourage employee acceptance and understanding. By developing training programs reflecting an à la carte mentality, associates can choose the right training classes targeted at their individual needs. In addition, these modular classes can continue to build on existing knowledge by identifying prerequisite classes required before more in-depth classes are attended.

Not every associate is going to be a project lead or need to know how to create a control chart. Companies therefore focus much of their efforts on teaching associates simple ways to make a difference with Six Sigma. By starting with basic tools such as CTQs, project plans, and process maps, employees at any level can implement change. In addition, training efforts focused on teaching customer-centric thinking are beneficial. Furthermore, understanding the relationships between quality and customer satisfaction results in engaged process owners, team members, and employees.

Alternatives to the Classroom

While classroom training provides the best method for coaching associates on the Six Sigma methodology, other methods can be effective and far less costly.

Distributing off-the-shelf books (like this one) throughout the various levels of an organization can provide associates with a window into the world of Six Sigma. Including Six Sigma terminology in group presentation materials and even status meetings can promote learning in an organization. One company even changed the name *status meeting* to *tollgate review* everywhere in the organization.

Company websites are a great place for sharing learning materials. Companies usually provide quick tidbits or did-you-know pieces for the front page to entice the associate into wanting to learn more. Company newsletters can also incorporate Six Sigma learning.

Saying Thanks

The investment in training and certification of associates can be great. For this reason, retaining these associates is critical for continued business success. In addition, getting associates to enter the belt program or participate as team members on projects can require persuasion. However, the more they participate, the more they understand the value of Six Sigma and the better equipped they will be to solve business problems.

So how do companies get people interested and keep them involved? Usually, the same tactics can accomplish both. They begin by sharing the victories. This includes …

- Communicating project successes in real dollars.
- Delivering quotes from process owners and people affected by the positive changes.
- Posting the results in break rooms, elevators, company websites, and newsletters.
- Naming names, including the belts and team members' names, whenever possible.
- Exposure to company executives through project presentations.

Project completion awards, such as plaques and certificates, are additional ways to show praise and gain momentum for Six Sigma. Annual award ceremonies are another way to celebrate Six Sigma success. On a less formal level, company meetings can be used as the backdrop for presenting these awards. The award ceremonies should always include project presentations, which encourage employees to discuss discoveries that will entice others to want to learn more.

Process Pointers

A personal letter from the CEO of your company to project leads and team members is a meaningful, low-cost way to say thanks.

Some companies may even provide monetary rewards for project completions and certification milestones. While this is not typically going to be a cut of the project savings (although wouldn't that be nice!), the rewards might come in the form of company stock, stock option grants, or possibly a promotion involving a salary increase.

Eliminating Culture Shock

So how do you encourage participation in a brand new program? How can an organization get past the old adage "this, too, shall pass" and convince employees that Six Sigma is here to stay?

The simplest way is by making them accountable for project completions. By establishing participation requirements in individual performance metrics either at a team level, lead level, or executive level, employees ultimately have no choice but to embrace the program and give it a try! Once they try it, they will like it.

We know that a major roadblock for participation is taking the time out of an already hectic schedule to sign up and attend training. We also know that associates may not always recognize the value of Six Sigma training and the associated participation in a project that it provides. For these reasons, we encourage companies to incorporate Six Sigma training goals and project delivery requirements for each associate into their performance development plans.

By creating specific learning objectives for each associate, associates can identify the right classes or belt level to enhance their current knowledge. They also will understand how Six Sigma training is related to their overall development.

The performance measurements can start with the simple requirements of attending training classes as identified in the goals section of a performance evaluation. If Six Sigma training goals for the company are established, these goals can easily be handed down to all levels of the organization and displayed for each individual in writing.

Other development metrics can be used to encourage team participation by identifying a minimum number of Six Sigma projects on which to participate that are easily accomplished within the evaluation timeframe.

Process Pointers

Encourage team leaders to provide feedback to team members' managers throughout the project. This will result in better team participation and encourage both positive and negative feedback to the team member.

The key is to make Six Sigma a responsibility of every associate in the company. By defining specific responsibilities for each individual associate—tracking progress and providing incentives and consequences for meeting or not meeting the predetermined goals—you will see success from holding people accountable for adopting Six Sigma.

The Least You Need to Know

- Look for leadership qualities, first and foremost, when selecting belts.
- Master black belts, black belts, and green belts have a similar certification process across companies.
- Companies typically set a goal for the number of individuals to train along with the type of training to give them.
- Training programs should be focused on the needs of the audience.
- Use performance metrics to spread the adoption of Six Sigma throughout your organization.

Chapter 6

Living with Change

In This Chapter

- How to plan for change
- Common reasons for resistance
- How associates and supervisors can ease the transition
- What to do when multiple projects address the same business problem

Change is hard. Whether you are changing jobs, moving, or having a baby, adjusting to the new environment and varying responsibilities can be a challenge. This is also true when changes are made to a process you own or one in which you participate. So, when a Six Sigma team comes on the scene and makes a change in your area, adapting to this change can be difficult.

In this chapter, we are going to arm you with ideas to make accepting and living with the changes easier. We include helpful hints for project teams to use to avoid pain when the process is modified.

We also discuss typical reactions when changes occur and how project teams, process owners, and process members can help eliminate or reduce negative reactions.

Lastly, we explain what can happen when a process owner is in the middle of improving a process and a Six Sigma team enters the picture.

The Right Plan

Planning for change, or *change management*, is the best way a project team or change agent can eliminate pain and resistance when changes are implemented.

> **Sigma Sayings**
>
> **Change management** is the plan used to establish acceptance around a new process or organizational change that ultimately affects people.

Change management tasks should be detailed in a team's implementation plan created during the improve phase. However, a team should *never* wait until the improve phase to begin planning for change. Instead, steps to ease the transition during the improve phase actually start in the define phase and continue throughout the project.

The Team Talks

Selecting the right team members is the first step a project leader can take to begin to manage change. By including associates on the team who participate in or own the current process that is going to be changed, awareness and support for change can begin. People who will be affected by changes want to have a say in what those changes should be. By participating in the process of identifying the problem and proposing solutions to the problem, people will accept and adapt more easily to the changes upon implementation. After all, these are the people living and breathing the current process every day.

Team members drive change through communication. The team members are selected for a particular project because they represent various areas affected by the process. Therefore, they have the important task of communicating back to their respective groups. A team lead can encourage this by providing materials that can be forwarded easily to associates outside the core team. For instance, a tollgate review document may be great for associates who have completed Six Sigma training, but an alternate version might be helpful for associates who do not yet understand the Six Sigma terminology.

In addition, the team lead should follow up during team meetings to determine which members are effectively spreading the information, and thus, creating the environment for change. The purpose of the follow-up is two-fold. First, this is a great way to solicit responses to the project. A team lead can often avoid roadblocks in the future just by asking a few simple questions:

- Are the associates energized that the problem is being addressed?
- Are the associates surprised by the initial findings?
- Do the associates believe the goal is realistic?

Second, by following up with team members to ensure communication is occurring, team leads can avoid surprises and responses such as, "I didn't know this was happening," which can inhibit the team's willingness to change.

It Really Does Hurt

Nothing increases pain more than implementing a revised process with problems in it. Because humans lead projects, mistakes are bound to happen. However, minimizing these mistakes is the responsibility of the project lead. By understanding in detail how things are currently accomplished, the team is more likely to identify and plan for all inherent changes the new process will bring about. For instance, if a system used in a process is being replaced, and a particular report produced by the old system is overlooked when the new system is implemented, the users of the report may reject the new system completely because a critical task was overlooked. Manual as well as automated processes must be understood to insure the new process is accepted. Leave no stone unturned! If not done properly, this type of change could deter others from accepting further changes, often needed for continuous improvement.

Process Pointers

The creation of procedure documents and job descriptions is critical to understanding responsibilities and roles. These are typically known as *standard operating procedures* or *SOPs*. When these documents are not updated to reflect the changes in the process, resistance to the new process or change can occur.

Any new or revised process typically requires the definition of new or revised roles and responsibilities. When finite details are ignored, such as who is assigned to perform the task and how the task is performed, the end result is confusion, which can result in chaos. “That’s not my job anymore” or “I don’t know who is supposed to do that” are common responses when new processes are poorly defined.

To Teach or Not to Teach

Developing effective training materials along with a strong training strategy is critical to planning for change. Training materials should be targeted toward each individual audience and focused on new or revised manual and automated procedures. For instance, an executive or senior management team may only require higher-level, results-focused materials, whereas associates, who live day-in and day-out with the new procedures or processes, may require more in-depth materials.

Process Pointers

When technology is added to a process, classroom training is usually the best approach to winning over associates.

If training classes are administered to assist with the acceptance of change, role-playing and real-life examples are critical to ensure audience members understand the topics at hand. In addition, soliciting feedback prior to the end of the class can be used to determine whether the objectives of the class were well-received. Feedback can be in the form of surveys or even tests to monitor the effectiveness of the class.

In some cases, the facilitation of change may not warrant formal training classes. Alternatives to an instructor-led training class might include the following:

- Online training
- Distributing detailed documents with instructions
- One-on-one desk-side training
- Presentation of a new process in an assembly format

However, using only one of these approaches can cause problems. Associates are great at ignoring or deleting e-mails regarding new procedures or avoiding assembly meetings when they have other priorities. Instead, a combination of these approaches is helpful to ensure the learning curve and the associated resistance to change will be minimized. Again, solicit feedback to gauge the effectiveness of the training.

Every training strategy should define how support for the new process will be handled and, most importantly, how the support group will be trained. Additional support associates are typically needed during the initial transition to a new process. For instance, if a new check acceptance procedure is implemented, the current help desk may need to plan for additional staffing during the first few months the cashiers use the new procedure.

A required component to any training strategy is conducting a pulse check: How is everyone doing? Was training effective? What is working and not working? The training strategy should identify when and how these pulse checks are conducted. Pulse checks can be in the form of conversations, meetings, surveys, or even spot checks on work performed. Don't be surprised to discover additional training is required after completing a pulse check.

Too Much Going On

Lastly, planning for change includes knowing about and planning around other changes affecting the associates. This includes systems or processes that might be rolling out simultaneously with the Six Sigma process change. It might also be an influx of new personnel joining the group or major organizational changes just announced. When associates are hit with too many changes all at once, their ability to adopt and comprehend the changes diminishes. In some cases, implementations of Six Sigma solutions may need to be delayed or rolled out more slowly because too many other things are going on at the same time within the organization.

So how can a team find out about potential changes to their environment? Staying close to the process owner and asking the right questions is a start. In addition, the project champion, who is typically the executive in charge of the area, alerts a project lead to potential changes occurring simultaneously.

Common Resistance

Sometimes the best-laid plans still don't achieve the best results. This means that even if a team has created the perfect process and the perfect implementation plan, some people will still resist the changes. This can result in poor morale and, in some cases, high turnover after the process changes are implemented.

The most common reason for resistance occurs due to one of the following:

- Associates don't understand the changes.
- Associates don't believe the data driving the changes.
- Associates felt uninvolved in the decision-making process.

When resistance occurs after implementation, the best way to overcome this is by altering the method of communication used previously and, in some cases, *over*-communicating. While it's often impossible to include every associate affected by the process change in the decision-making process, a project team can help keep large numbers of associates in the loop with verbal and written communication, memos, and voicemails. By attending status meetings and monthly or quarterly functional meetings, a team member or lead can usually take a few seconds to provide an update on the project. This is a great way to reach a large number of associates who will later be affected by the change.

If circumstances exist where communication can only occur at the end of a project (that is, during training), the project lead should attempt to share details on how the solution was achieved, who was involved in selecting the solution, and what testing occurred before the solution was implemented. Leads should never expect that just because they are the lead, they no longer have an obligation to the associates affected by the change to explain *why* the changes are occurring. Actually, the opposite is true. Explaining *why* to all associates will ease the transition and promote acceptance in the long run. When people know the facts and understand the data, they more readily adapt to the changes.

Defect Alert

In some cases, the best method of communication with resistant associates is a one-on-one meeting. Taking the time to address the concerns head-on often dispels the concerns. The meetings should be designed to understand what is causing the resistance. Using questions rather than presenting answers creates more productive meetings. For instance, asking "Why do you have issues?" along with "What do you suggest we do to address the issues?" can help identify and create solutions for the opposition.

A project team, above all, should listen to the conflicted associates. If ignored, serious problems might arise. Low morale can result in unproductive associates. This type of behavior might affect quality in the short term, with incomplete or poorly performed tasks. In the long term, the effect will be seen in high turnover rates. High turnover is a cost most companies would rather prevent.

Still, making everyone happy is not the responsibility of the Six Sigma team. In many cases, it's impossible anyway. Some Six Sigma solutions might result in the elimination of positions or the reassignment of job duties. People involved in these types of decisions are not going to be overjoyed for obvious reasons. When the elimination of jobs occurs, the team should focus on ensuring selections are just. The team should work closely with the legal and human resources areas to ensure that company policies, along with state and federal laws, are upheld. In addition, all groups affected, including associates indirectly affected by the changes, should be presented with the details of the project that shaped this end result.

Keep in mind, the primary goal of the Six Sigma project team is to make certain the results eliminate the root cause and don't create additional problems. By testing new solutions and communicating the results, the team will be one step closer to success.

Making It Better

So what can you do if you are affected by changes resulting from a Six Sigma implementation? How can you eliminate the sting? The best thing to do is be positive. Having a positive attitude creates an environment for open communication. As communication resonates, you can gain a deeper understanding of why the changes are being made. When you understand the data that led to the changes, you will begin to support the changes.

If you are having problems adjusting to changes within your area, take the initiative to ask questions. It's okay to demand project details as long as you do it in a positive way. Focus on asking the following questions based on your understanding of Six Sigma:

- What was the initial goal of the project?
- What was the baseline result?
- What root causes were found?
- What tests were performed to select the primary solution?
- What controls have been put in place to sustain the solution?

Another way to help out a project team is by being open to new ideas and new ways of doing things. Steer away from the old adage, "Well, we've never done it that way in the past, so it just won't work." This won't help stop the changes nor will it help make the changes easier to tolerate. Instead, listen to the project team, review any data available, and understand the steps they took to develop the solution. By all means, if they missed something or a true problem exists, don't hesitate to discuss the issues with the team. However, if you are going to bring up problems, make sure you provide recommendations as well.

Finally, you can make it better by being responsive. If you are invited to participate in training, reviews, or presentations, make every effort to attend. Don't complain during implementation that you were not kept in the loop when you actually chose not to participate.

Supervising the Change

If you are in charge of a group affected by Six Sigma changes, you can also help manage the change. Your direct reports are going to count on you to support the new process. The best way to show support is to partner with the team and take ownership of any communication going out to your group. Announcing the changes and participating in or even leading any new training are two great ways to display approval for the new process.

As the primary point of contact for the Six Sigma team, your number one goal is to communicate the changes as quickly as possible. Keep your direct reports in the loop, even if bad news is on the way. This is a great way to prevent rumors and inaccurate information from spreading.

Motivating direct reports is important for any manager or supervisor. It becomes especially important when Six Sigma implementations occur. This is when creativity comes in handy. Incentives can be a great motivator. For instance, if an associate's responsibilities are shifting, offer rewards to encourage a quick and smooth transition. Remember, rewards don't have to be monetary. These can be in the form of a certificate, recognition during an assembly meeting, or a complimentary written note attached to a performance review.

When Conflicts Arise

Sometimes a Six Sigma team is selected to work on a problem that a group or process owner is already addressing through the use of non–Six Sigma methods. This can place a Six Sigma lead in a difficult situation. Not only will a Six Sigma team face resistance from the process owner in this case, they might also experience some difficulty acquiring resources for the project.

Because Six Sigma project definitions should be in line with corporate goals and strategy, it makes sense that a team lead might find the process owner already in the midst of trying to solve the same problem presented to the Six Sigma team. Clearly, if a corporate metric is not being achieved, a good process owner will feel the pain early and begin addressing the business concern to the best of their ability.

Sometimes, the process owner is only addressing surface-level problems as they arise while waiting for a more-thorough Six Sigma project to begin. In other cases, new corporate systems may be rolling out that affect the process by default. If the process owner is new to the company or new to Six Sigma, they might be utilizing another approach to solving the business problem.

So what should a project team do when this occurs? Well, the worst thing it can do is go in and try to put a stop to other projects addressing the same issue. Instead, a Six Sigma team lead should work closely with the process owner to have them join and support the new project. Remember, the process owner is a critical participant in any Six Sigma project.

Defect Alert

If other projects addressing the same business problem result in solutions that directly conflict with the Six Sigma project team's solution, use open communication with the process owner and teams to present clear data-based findings.

Next, the team lead should solicit feedback and ongoing communication about the other project(s) addressing the issue. This enables the team to stay abreast of changes occurring within the process as the Six Sigma team begins to measure the current process and identify solutions. The most challenging part of working on a Six Sigma project while other changes are occurring is that the current process becomes a moving target. With a moving target, the team has to put a stake in the ground to measure. From this point on, the team needs to maintain a list of changes occurring that might affect solution testing down the road.

For instance, assume a Six Sigma team is tasked with reducing the cycle time for a bill-paying process and another project implements a new system to automate steps of the process. If the initial measure was completed prior to the new system implementation, the team will likely have to complete an additional measure to exclude the amount of cycle time reduction that resulted due to the new system. By avoiding the additional measure, the results of the new solution may present an inflated benefit stream.

In some cases, a Six Sigma team lead has to decide whether to postpone a Six Sigma project until the process owner has completed the project underway. Usually, this occurs when resources are limited or changes from the existing projects are large and the estimated timeframe for implementing the changes are lengthy. By postponing the Six Sigma project, a team can be more productive in measuring the newly revised process to determine what, if any, enhancements are needed.

The Least You Need to Know

- Planning for change begins during the define phase of a Six Sigma project.
- Selecting the right team members and creating an effective new process helps eliminate resistance to change.
- Implementation strategies should take into account other changes, including organizational, process, and systems, which are affecting the same process group.
- When other projects are focused on the same business problem, stay abreast of the changes to ensure conflicts between the projects don't arise.

Chapter 7

Join in the Fun

In This Chapter

- How teams are formed
- What to expect when participating on a project team
- The project lead's responsibilities to the team members
- Functioning as a team
- Why you should join a team

You've been asked to join a project team and you just don't know what to say. Participating on a Six Sigma team can be an exciting adventure. While project leads act as change agents, team members are the people who truly define and implement the final changes.

However, when your boss or coworker asks you to join a project, you need to understand what to expect. Although participating on a team can be rewarding, it can also be a challenging experience. In this chapter, we discuss how team members are selected and describe what a team leader will expect from you if and when you join the team.

Finally, if you've ever participated on project teams in the past, you probably know that no two team leaders or teams are alike. We prepare you for joining a Six Sigma team by providing you with a list of what you should expect from your team leader and explain the unique transition a typical team faces as it moves from concept to action.

Team Selection

Chances are you were not selected for a team based on your looks. Instead, you probably touch some part of a process that needs improvement. Selecting the right team members often requires a project leader to anticipate all the functional areas touching the current broken process along with those areas that might touch the future process.

Another reason you might have been selected for a particular project is that you're good with numbers, people, communication, technology, or data. Often, project leads include participants from the finance, human resources, and information technology departments to round out the skill set of a team.

A representative from the finance organization can provide validation and support of key metrics, goals, and identified projected savings. In addition, any costs and benefits identified can be reviewed to ensure the format and criteria match that of your organization.

Process Pointers

If you are selected for a team that does not include a representative from finance and information technology, make a recommendation to your manager to insure these folks are added to the team.

Likewise, an IT resource can come in handy throughout the project. Because data is such a strong factor in establishing metrics, baselines, and goals, an IT resource can help in selecting the right solution. In addition, they can help identify what data exists and where to go to get it as well as help analyze the data results. An IT resource also can tell you how data was calculated (if produced electronically) or where the data came from.

Defect Alert

Often, a new process developed during the improve phase may require new or modified technology. Make sure someone from the IT group is included as a team member or stakeholder to assist the team in identifying or implementing technology.

In addition to IT personnel, you might also find suppliers and customers on your project team.

These are great assets to include on a team. Customers can provide valuable insight into the problem at hand while vendors might identify roadblocks to potential solutions.

What Is Expected

In the end, implementing changes as a team member can be very rewarding. However, getting to the end result and coming up with the right solution takes effort on your part. Project success is directly related to the level of effort provided by team members. The more team members participate, the better the result. However, team members typically have other responsibilities and priorities outside of the project on which they are participating. Therefore, balancing life on a team with life in your regular job can be difficult. This is why it's important to understand what is required before you agree to participate on a team. If you agree to be on a team, you should …

- Attend regular team meetings.
- Be open to new ideas.
- Actively participate in team discussions.
- Be a communication champion.
- Complete tasks on time.

Attendance

Attending team meetings sounds pretty easy. However, it never fails when a last-minute project is thrown in your lap, a meeting with your boss is called, or you get a call from school and one of your kids is sick. All of these reasons require you to call your project lead and cancel. The problem with canceling is that, usually, the agenda of the meeting requires attendance from all participants for the meeting to be successful. For instance, if the task at hand for today's meeting is to create a cause-and-effect diagram, one team member's absence could result in key causes being overlooked.

Defect Alert

In some cases, you just can't avoid missing a meeting. If you know far enough in advance, your team lead might be able to reschedule the meeting or select another topic to address while you are out. Furthermore, your team lead may be able to get some of your insight before the meeting for later use.

If, due to the time constraints of the project, your lead must complete the task at hand, you might select another representative from your area to participate. Just be sure the person you select has knowledge of the project and at least some knowledge of Six Sigma. We also encourage you to submit any special considerations related to the meeting topic to your team lead prior to the meeting. Most importantly, follow-up with your team lead after the meeting. If you selected a substitute to attend the meeting, ask them to take detailed notes on the outcome. In some cases, your project lead will also submit notes following team meetings.

Be Open

Even if you didn't come up with an idea, keep an open mind when participating in team meetings. Feel free to ask plenty of questions, so you have an easier time understanding the reasoning behind others' suggestions. Listen to your teammates and hear what they have to say. Often, we find team members lack this important skill, known as effective listening.

As a team member, you also must be open to change. Keep in mind that a better way might exist. Just because you always did things a certain way in the past does not mean that process was effective. This is why your Six Sigma team was formed in the first place—to correct processes that are creating undesired results.

Some of the best ideas start off as silly ideas, so be creative and innovative to ensure all ideas are presented. For example, in a plant where too much inventory was kept, one of the associates suggested they should just take out some of the shelving so the inventory wouldn't pile up. The project lead loved the idea and removed some of the shelving. Soon thereafter, the excess inventory was reduced because the people ordering the material had no place to store the excess.

Silly ideas many times are in the form of "just stop doing it that way." This is similar to "if it hurts when you do *that*, stop doing *that*." For example, a great deal of confusion existed around ordering product from a supplier. The supplier would take fax, phone calls, e-mails, and web orders. Many times there was duplication and rework. When the project lead took over, the team made a recommendation to stop taking orders in so many different ways. The project lead said, "You're right" and reduced all orders to phone calls or web only.

Participate, Participate, Participate

Don't be a fly on the wall in group settings. Engage other team members. Make suggestions and provide feedback to your facilitator. If you don't understand something, ask questions. Usually, other team members also don't understand but are afraid to speak up.

As you learn Six Sigma, the simplest question you can ask is, "What is the defect?" A follow-up question could be, "What process are we attacking?"

Still, don't overdo it. Often team members like to disagree just to disagree. If you do disagree with a recommendation or solution, provide constructive feedback. Make sure the points you address are well thought out. It's always best to support your ideas with examples and data.

By sharing your experiences, you create a learning environment among your team members that enhances the team's overall cohesiveness. The right balance of participation from all team members creates excellent information-sharing resulting in effective problem-solving.

Champion Communication

If you are selected for a team, one of the reasons may be that the area to which you belong is going to be affected by the changes to come. Therefore, the more you discuss details of the project with other people from your area, the easier time your team will have when it's time to implement changes.

A great way to keep everyone informed is to provide regular updates during your normal status meetings or meeting updates with your boss. Keep these project snapshots short and sweet. Don't overwhelm your functional group members with information overload. Your primary objective is to keep them in the loop on the direction and status of the project along with any key results or decisions made.

Defect Alert

Avoid using too much Six Sigma jargon in your project updates. This is not a time to show how much you know about Six Sigma, but rather, how much your team has accomplished with the use of Six Sigma.

Championing communication is also a great way to help your company spread Six Sigma learning. As you keep non–team members abreast of your project with tollgates, you are teaching fellow associates various terms and tasks inherent in a Six Sigma project.

Let your co-workers know what phase of the project you are working on. Discuss current Sigma levels and goals for improvement. Most important, share the vision of the improve phase of the project. Get feedback on the process changes your team has identified and use the data to support it.

Are You Done Yet?

Your project lead can't do everything alone. Completing the project on time requires commitment and dedication from each team member. The last thing a project lead wants to do is baby-sit the team.

When you join a team, you are asked to assist in various tasks throughout the life of the project. For instance, you might be asked to …

- Create or administer interview questions for customers.
- Call other companies for a benchmarking exercise.
- Execute a test of the measure system developed.
- Stratify data.
- Compile survey results.

Regardless of the task you are assigned to, don't be late! Know the expected completion date for your tasks. If you anticipate conflicts with other assignments, communicate them early to your team leader. The team leader may be able to shift around assignments to better fit your schedule.

Still, the best-laid plans don't always work out. If you take on an assignment and find you are unable to complete the assignment on time, look for help within the team or even within your functional area. Just be sure to review the work if it is completed by someone else to ensure accuracy.

What to Command

Pulling together a part-time team and managing this team through the completion of the project can be a difficult task for even the greatest leader. Because team members typically have other job responsibilities, a project lead must be sure not to waste a team member's valuable time. So, just as a project lead will have certain expectations of you, if you join a team, you should have certain expectations of your project lead.

Expectations of a project lead include …

- Being a good facilitator.
- Having a plan.
- Gaining executive support.
- Providing team training.

Defect Alert

When your team lead falls short of one or more of the predefined expectations, good team members will confront their leader and provide constructive feedback. This should be accomplished in a one-on-one conversation. Avoid the use of e-mail or group discussions when providing this feedback.

Good Facilitation

Your team lead or facilitator must know how to keep people energized. He or she must demonstrate the ability to get everyone involved. If one person in a meeting is not participating, your lead should know how to draw the team member into the discussion.

A good facilitator conducts organized meetings. The development of meeting agendas along with the identification of clear goals and objectives provides the team with clear direction and results in making things happen!

Upon completion of a meeting, the facilitator should also document and distribute a meeting summary.

Process Pointers

Listening effectively is not only an important quality for you and your team to have, but it is also an expectation you should have of your team leader. Respect is obtained by encouraging effective listening throughout the team. Without mutual respect, the team is destined for failure.

Facilitators also need to know how to keep meetings moving. If your group is getting stuck on one topic and has difficulty agreeing on a resolution, a strong facilitator will move the meeting along by either setting another time to investigate and resolve the issue or by making a majority-based decision. You and your team should expect meetings to end on time.

Finally, your leader should present his or her experiences when appropriate. Chances are he or she has done something similar in the past or has examples from other companies or teams. Your leader didn't get to be the team lead by accident! However, a good team leader will steer clear of influencing the team in one direction or another based on these experiences.

Charting the Course

Having a plan is the only way to keep your team on track. As we mentioned earlier, a project charter is key to organizing and directing a successful project. As a team member, you should insist on understanding the goals, objectives, and general timeline for the project.

In addition, a set of detailed tasks should be presented to the team at the start of each DMAIC phase. Think of this as the roadmap for each phase. By knowing when and how you will be needed throughout the phase, you can better balance your time between this Six Sigma project and your other responsibilities.

Process Pointers

Setting a predefined meeting day and time for the life of the project often eases the burden of scheduling. If the meeting time is not needed based on the point of the project, your lead can always cancel the time. This is also how your tollgate reviews should be scheduled.

Life on a project is ever-changing. Project sponsors may come and go. Team members may be replaced. Business needs might change. Whatever the reason for change, your project lead should revise the project plan as needed and redistribute it to the team.

Executive Ear

A good team lead will have the ear of an executive sponsor at regular intervals throughout the project. You don't want to reach the end of the improve phase to find out that a project or executive sponsor is not onboard with the results from your measure phase or has issues with how you defined the original project goal.

In some cases, team members might accompany the lead to an executive overview meeting, but this is not always possible. If you are unable to attend one of these critical meetings, your lead should provide documented feedback for the team. Also, you can request a preview of the information to be presented at the meeting. Keep in mind, your name is on the charter and the team's results are a reflection of your work. Likewise, as a team member, your name is also on the charter, showing your participation and agreement to actions.

Knowledge Is Everything

If this is your first Six Sigma project, you should expect to be trained on the DMAIC (define, measure, analyze, improve, and control) process before your project begins. By understanding the primary process and tools of Six Sigma, you will be a more valuable team participant.

Your lead might choose to accomplish this training in one of the following ways:

- Administer overview and detailed training at the start of the project.

- Administer overview training during a project kickoff and provide additional detailed training throughout each phase of the project.
- Send the team to a class taught by a certified instructor inside or outside the company.

Whichever method of training is selected, understanding the basics of Six Sigma will enhance your experience on the project.

Team Dynamics

Just as you might have grown up having a love-hate relationship with your siblings, you are sure to have a love-hate relationship with your teammates. This, too, is healthy. Because your team members all represent different areas of the broken process, you might have different views on why the process is broken and how it should be fixed. These differences of opinion sometimes result in conflicts within the team, especially in a newly formed team. As your team continues to work together, the conflicts usually weaken.

Because teams play such an important role in the success of Six Sigma projects, we believe it's helpful to understand how teams operate. The most popular model describing team performance was created in 1965 by Dr. Bruce Tuckman. His theory on team performance is still being taught in businesses and schools throughout the world.

Dr. Tuckman identified four stages of team performance. With awareness of these stages, you can help your team and team lead achieve a high-functioning team status. High-functioning teams ultimately produce better solutions than low functioning teams.

Forming

As a new team comes together, much emphasis is placed on the team leader. Tuckman describes this stage as *forming*.

In the forming stage, team members rely heavily on their leader for direction. They also use this early stage to test the waters and gain an understanding of other team members and how they might interact with one another. Team members tend to ask many questions during this time and digest as much knowledge related to the structure and process of the team as possible.

The good news is this generally occurs during the define phase of a Six Sigma project. Because this is the time the project lead is expected to provide most of the direction, few issues arise with the team members.

Storming

During the next stage of team performance, defined as *storming*, conflict is everywhere. Each team member is trying to find a place on the team where they might stand out and be noticed. Usually, this results in ineffective listening or even a lack of active participation in meetings.

Although your team is beginning to understand the purposes and goals of the project, they are still focusing on their individual needs rather than the needs of the group as a whole.

If your team stays in this stage for too long, the team lead might need to initiate team training in an effort to educate individuals on the responsibilities and expectations of team members.

Your goal as a team is to get out of this phase before completing the measure phase of Six Sigma.

Norming

Some teams will reach the *norming* stage and remain there throughout most of the Six Sigma project. This is a good place to be as your team is making decisions cohesively and displaying respect for each other and your team leader.

During this stage, your team leader moves into a facilitation role while the team takes charge and ownership of the tactical direction of the project. It is during this stage that effective brainstorming sessions and consensus building can begin to occur.

Some teams tend to move back and forth between the storming and norming stages.

Performing

The last stage of a team is *performing*. This is the ultimate team. A performing team is focused on project strategy and requires very little involvement from the team leader. This team knows how to work together to accomplish its goals. They act as one voice and support each other effectively.

Process Pointers

If your team reaches a performing stage and you are completing the project, you might consider keeping the team intact to focus on related process problems that were out of the scope of the original project.

Not every Six Sigma team reaches the performing stage quickly. As a matter of fact, not every team reaches this stage. Even the best teams can take six months or more to attain the performing status. In most cases, a Six Sigma project is completed before your team can reach the performing stage.

Benefits of Joining

Well, so far it sounds like a lot of work needs to be done when participating on a team. So why would anyone doing well in his or her current position want to rock the boat?

First of all, not everyone gets the choice. As discussed earlier, in most cases, you are selected to be on a team by your boss based on the needs of the project. In addition, you or your boss might be looking for additional opportunities to enhance or further develop your existing talents. Whatever the case for selection, there are plenty of advantages for you.

By participating on a Six Sigma team, you gain insight into how to solve problems systematically and effectively. You learn from an experienced project lead how to create and execute a project plan. Understanding how to develop goals and objectives is another positive reason for your effective participation.

Your involvement also expands your ability to communicate effectively as a project member. From participating in team meetings to reviewing project documentation and creating executive overview materials, you will improve your written and verbal communication. No matter what position you hold in your company, this skill alone will help you go far.

Last but not least, you gain practical experience from using the Six Sigma toolset. As you may recall, these tools can be used throughout Six Sigma to improve anything from the smallest of problems to large-scale, multi-tiered issues.

All of the skills we mentioned are what separate managers from leaders in an organization. The more projects you participate in, the more likely you will be asked to take on a project leadership role as Six Sigma grows and expands throughout your company. So, if you are asked to join in the fun of a Six Sigma project, your first response should be, "When do I start?"

The Least You Need to Know

- Team members should actively participate in team discussions and be open to new ideas.
- Team leaders should have strong facilitation skills.
- Most teams go through four primary stages: forming, storming, norming, and performing.
- Participation on a Six Sigma team can help you develop leadership skills for future opportunities within your organization.

Accepting the Lead

In This Chapter

- Recommending Six Sigma projects in your organization
- Things to consider before becoming a belt
- Ways to increase your chances of being selected to lead a project
- Transforming Six Sigma to meet the needs of your organization

Six Sigma has a way of making everyone in your organization a leader. By educating associates on how to spot quality issues and empowering them to fix problems, new leaders will emerge.

This chapter shows you clever ways to build and demonstrate your leadership skills as Six Sigma is adopted in your organization. If you are considering a position as a green belt or black belt, we tell you what things to consider, as well as provide you with tips for developing yourself for one of these positions.

We also talk about the changes that occur within organizations when they make the commitment to adopt Six Sigma completely.

Daily Dosage

So, you haven't been asked to be on a project, but you want to get more involved in Six Sigma. How can you take the initiative to expand your Six Sigma knowledge and utilize it while you remain in your current position?

Finding Problems

A great way to show your boss what you have learned is to recommend projects to drive improvements. Six Sigma project ideas can come from almost anywhere. Many originate when an executive fears he is not meeting a number or metric outlined during his performance plan. Others result from customer complaints. Still, employees remain the best source for identifying problems in a company.

As an employee in a Six Sigma organization, you should always be on the lookout for things that are broken. You might find expenses that should be reduced, product quality issues arising, or processes taking too long. Sometimes, an area with undefined roles or overlapping responsibilities screams out for help.

Process Pointers

If you believe a problem exists but don't have enough data to present a baseline, focus on setting up a measuring system to capture a baseline for use in a future Six Sigma project. Many projects will come from the hunches of management or corporate leaders that an ongoing issue is occurring. This is sometimes a reaction to a single event, or a low sample size. For instance, if a manager receives one complaint from a customer and assumes the complaints are widespread, the manager should collect more data to verify or invalidate that the defect exists.

Some questions you might ask when looking for a project are:

- Is the process or output important to the business?
- Do metrics exist?
- How much data exists and how hard will it be to collect additional data?
- Is there an advantage to improving the process, such as customer satisfaction or immediate financial benefits?
- Will the solution require information technology modifications?

Even if you are unsure whether your current opportunity or defect is a green belt or black belt project, don't hesitate to submit the potential project recommendations. In some cases, companies have an internal website for idea generation. Other companies might use more informal methods, such as manually making suggestions to managers and executives. Still, it is usually a good idea to present ideas to your boss first. Even though other activities outside your area may be occurring to address the project you plan to recommend, you should always look to submit ideas. Also, by showing the initiative, your boss may think of you next time a Six Sigma project lead is needed.

If Six Sigma is new to your organization and a method for submitting project ideas does not yet exist, take the lead in contacting a master black belt to recommend the project. Be sure to go armed with ideas and maybe even a helpful process map representing how the new process could work.

Don't forget, very few, if any, projects require the use of all Six Sigma tools to implement a sustainable solution. Understanding the basic Six Sigma tools discussed in this book enables you to take steps toward doing things better and improving processes.

Expand Your Horizons

The best leaders don't wait to be taught. Leaders take the initiative to identify topics that will promote growth and focus on acquiring as much information and expertise in an area of interest as possible.

By reading this book, you are already on the way to expanding your knowledge of Six Sigma. However, there is more you can do.

If Six Sigma has been in your company for a while, you can begin by reading about projects that have already made a difference. Sometimes these can be found on company websites. Otherwise, you might have to contact someone from your Six Sigma organization to request project documentation. After you've found it, focus on the approach used to solving the problem, as well as the tools selected to measure, test, and validate. This information will give you ideas for recommending projects and further enhance your understanding of the Six Sigma process.

Training classes are another way to learn more about Six Sigma. Talk to your boss about creating an individual training plan to broaden your knowledge and use of Six Sigma. Depending on your organization, some of these classes may be internal, but you might also be able to take classes outside your organization. Partner with a master black belt in your company to identify classes and instructors that meet your needs.

Of course, the Internet and your local bookstore are great sources for Six Sigma learning. Many companies post their successes on their intranet for all to use as a method to communicate Six Sigma results. In addition, some websites exist to educate associates about the benefits of Six Sigma. Your local bookstore is also filled with Six Sigma materials aimed at every audience.

Go to Work

If you really want to take a leadership role in Six Sigma, you should just start fixing things by meeting with current belts and champions to begin applying some of the methodology. You don't have to be on a project to fix things. The best place to start is within your own area. If you identified and submitted project ideas as discussed previously, ask your boss if you can take one of the ideas and use what you've learned to fix the problem. You can also start small by selecting one or two tools learned and incorporating them into your daily life. Using process maps, charters, and project work plans are great ways to get you ready for a Six Sigma leadership role.

Lastly, make your interest known. If you want to join a project team, make sure your boss is aware of that. In some cases, your boss can recommend you to participate on projects outside your area if your area has no existing projects. However, this is unlikely. As an employee of your company, you are encouraged, if not required, to improve the processes you own. You can always look to do things faster, with better quality, or with reduced costs. Remember, however, that you should not sacrifice one improvement at the expense, or loss, of another. For example, when reducing cycle time, be sure that your quality level does not decrease.

To Be or Not to Be a Belt

After taking a few classes and participating on a team, you've caught the bug. You think you want to take on more but you're just not sure. How do you decide whether or not becoming a belt is right for you? The best way to start is by leading a small project. In some cases, this might be a green belt project, but other companies have additional levels of belts, like orange or white. The difference between the belts is typically the level of training required to lead the project along with the size of the project defined.

In many cases, an associate is selected for a belt position. So, if you are selected, can you really say "no"? Probably not. After a company makes the decision to invest in Six Sigma, it begins to use Six Sigma leadership and experience as criteria for advancement. This means you should take advantage of all opportunities to further your Six Sigma knowledge. Turning down a belt position might restrict your career goals in the future.

Being selected to lead a project can be both an honor and a fright. It is an honor because your boss thinks you have the know-how to lead a project. Yet, it is a fright because you now have a project to lead. And you probably have other responsibilities in addition to the project. Unless you are a black belt, you are going to be expected to complete the Six Sigma project on top of your normal, everyday job.

Don't worry. With strong organization skills, the right team, and the right project definition, you won't have to burn the midnight oil. Begin by identifying how much time you can realistically spend on the new project. Review your workload list and determine whether lower priority items exist that can wait until the Six Sigma project is complete.

Process Pointers

Typically, 20 percent of your time, or one day per week, should be allocated to a Six Sigma green belt project. We recommend you block out this day on your calendar to focus 100 percent on your project. Plan team meetings for this day, meet with your project sponsor, and work on completing documentation.

Also, make sure you utilize your team effectively. In particular, when leading a belt project, you will need to make assignments to your team members and follow up to ensure the tasks are completed on time. If you try to take on everything yourself, you will fail. Also, partner closely with your assigned mentor. This might be a black belt or master black belt. Use this resource to ensure you stay on track and apply the tools effectively. Set up regular meetings to make certain you are heading in the right direction.

If you are selected for a black belt position, you might be concerned about what will happen to your existing position. Because most black belt positions last two or more years, your existing position most likely will be filled permanently. Often, you are asked to train and mentor your replacement while beginning your new role as a black belt.

We have too often seen black belts fail to meet their deadlines due to the lingering of old job responsibilities. This can be challenging for even the best associates. Sometimes, the new black belt has difficulty passing the reigns to a replacement. Other times, the replacement continues to depend on the black belt for assistance in the new position. Whichever the case, the sooner you can break away from your old position, the more success you will have in your new position as a black belt.

From a leadership perspective, you can do one of two things to prevent the new black belt from being pulled back to their old responsibilities. One is to give the new black belt a workload that consumes all their time. A black belt should be able to start with two large projects and pick up others as they progress through the original two projects. The second is to have the black belt work projects in another area of the business. This helps divorce the new black belt from her old responsibilities and keeps the area replacement from depending on and distracting the new black belt. In both cases, the new black belt is accountable for deliverables that do not allow him or her to spend much time helping out on previous job responsibilities.

Getting Picked

If your company uses a Six Sigma candidate selection process, you might wonder what you can do to get your name added to the list. Companies, first and foremost, look for candidates who excel in their current positions. Usually, these associates have expressed an interest in taking on new challenges or their boss is looking for additional growth opportunities.

If your job performance ratings are top notch, prove yourself by volunteering to lead projects. These might be small projects within your area that aren't actually defined as Six Sigma projects. However, if you take ownership of a project and begin to apply some of the Six Sigma rigor, you will not only learn more about the value of the tools, but you'll also impress your boss with successful project results.

Another way you can stand out is by demonstrating a true focus on the customer. Know who your customer is and help your peers, boss, and direct reports stay in tune with your customer requirements. If you are participating on projects or working on assignments that don't keep the customer in the forefront, speak up and help guide others back to true customer-centric thinking.

Also, know your area well and express an interest in improving it. Most green belts are selected based on their functional knowledge within a particular area. However, if you don't show an openness to change and are resistant to acknowledging that improvements can be made, the chances of being selected are slim.

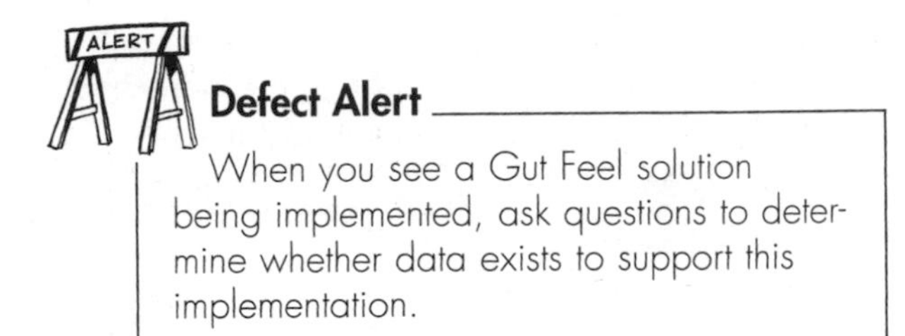

Defect Alert

When you see a Gut Feel solution being implemented, ask questions to determine whether data exists to support this implementation.

Some businesses look for the area of improvement first, then select a top candidate from the process owners in that area. To ensure you are identified as a top candidate in a critical area of the business, make sure you understand the processes in your area. You should also fully understand all impacts on the customer as well as the critical measures that are relative to customer expectation.

Life After Being a Belt

You made it on the list. You've been selected and served your time. Now what? What do green belts and black belts do next? This varies based on the following:

- Interest level of the belt
- Available positions within the company
- Level of experience of the belt

Some belts have an interest in pursuing Six Sigma permanently. This often leads to taking on a full-time black belt position as a stepping-stone to a master black belt position. After achieving the master black belt certification, associates can typically pursue a mentoring and coaching role, a permanent project lead role, or a combination of them.

If you are heading down the path of pursuing a full-time Six Sigma career, don't worry that you will be stuck forever. Many master black belts move on to executive level positions following several years of coaching and running Six Sigma projects. The experience gained is a perfect entry into managing large business units. In fact, we've seen master black belts become vice presidents and senior vice presidents of areas such as operations, product development, human resources, and information technology.

Most green belts will return to their everyday job because, as a green belt, they never really left it. However, they will approach their jobs in a very different way. The skills they developed while leading a green belt project are now applied back to every function they touch. This is how Six Sigma improves an employee's performance level. Chances are, the green belt associate will move on to more complex green belt projects and, in many cases, this green belt will be selected for increased job responsibilities, often resulting in promotional opportunities.

Black belts, on the other hand, do not typically have a position to which to return. In most cases, the position was filled when the black belt took on their new role. However, because black belt projects are typically large in scope and may cross multiple functional areas, the black belt will be introduced to many opportunities outside the belt's previous functional area. In addition, a black belt will develop contacts along the way that may lead to additional opportunities upon completion of their black belt tenure.

Process Pointers

Many companies assist black belts in finding positions by holding job fairs to enable black belts to learn about other areas and evaluate open positions. Hiring personnel often target these associates because of their proven success at improving processes along with the project management and analytical skills developed while leading black belt projects.

Many companies have utilized a career-fair type of in-placement process wherein the human resources vice president publishes a book that contains the accomplishments of the black belts. These books are distributed to all human resources managers and functional leaders, allowing them to look at the accomplishments of these future leaders.

Still, there is always the opportunity to return to your previous position. In some cases, the person who assumed your old role might be ready to experience Six Sigma first hand.

Whatever your interest, if you are selected for and agree to pursue a Six Sigma leadership role, as a successful black belt, you will find numerous options when you are ready to return to the organization. The key to a successful in-placement is to work closely with project champions and company officers to help improve their business with the implementation of sustainable solutions.

Reshaping Six Sigma to Fit Your Organization

During the past 25+ years that Six Sigma has been in existence, companies have adapted the methodology to fit their cultures and organizations. Six Sigma does not look the same everywhere, nor does it have to. Instead, Six Sigma leaders within various organizations have tailored the organizational structure, the project process, and even the toolset to meet the unique needs of the company as well as its culture.

Taking the lead in a Six Sigma organization requires thinking outside the box. When something inherent within the Six Sigma methodology doesn't appear to meld with the culture of your organization, a true leader will make recommendations for alterations.

Process Pointers

Six Sigma is often thought of as a tightly defined methodology because it mandates hard requirements for deliverables, tasks, structure, and time frames. However, many companies define variances from the stringent structure upon implementation to create consistency across the organization.

For instance, one large company mandated a two-month guideline for completing projects. This affected the method they used for scoping projects. Another company, due to its limited systems and data streams, opted for longer project durations of up to one year when they realized the collection of data might be more time consuming.

Creating common formats for deliverables, such as project charters, tollgate presentations, and process maps, also helps a company execute more useful training materials and maintain a common language. However, again, these formats will vary based on the needs of the company. For instance, some companies prefer the Six Sigma goal be identified only after an extensive gauge R&R test has been performed. Therefore, this information would not appear anywhere in the define phase tollgate. Other companies want the project lead to take a stab or best guess at the current Sigma to create a goal during the define phase.

Creating common formats is a great way to enforce the use of certain tools and tasks. If a measure tollgate presentation template has a page for gauge R&R test results, the project lead can view this as a requirement for the measure phase. Likewise, if a define tollgate template contains a page for the stakeholder analysis, this becomes a required document rather than a nice-to-have.

Mandates for savings levels also vary across companies. Some companies place a minimum dollar savings amount to be realized. Other companies allow for a certain percentage of projects to be focused on customer service initiatives rather than immediate hard-dollar benefits.

Many companies might incorporate other methodologies, either internally written or adopted from the outside, into the Six Sigma methodology. A popular term out there today for consultants is *Lean Sigma*. Most good Six Sigma programs have lean built in to the methodology.

Sigma Sayings

Lean Sigma is a term adopted from Motorola's lean manufacturing to refer to the elimination of waste. Waste is defined as loss of productivity, safety, inventory, and so on.

Other adaptations often added are project management and change management, which we discuss in Chapter 6, or company-specific initiatives, like adding strategic resource planning, operating requirements, or the inclusion of government regulations.

Changes can even be made to the standard DMAIC project management problem-solving strategy. For instance, one company added an *implementation* phase to the DMAIC methodology to create DMAIIC. While implementation is traditionally part of the improve phase, this particular company wanted to separate implementation from selection, piloting, and testing in order to track progress through the application of a separate tollgate.

Regardless of the type of project you are leading, don't assume the steps are hard-coded. Instead, just as you are now trained to make processes in your area better, continue to look for ways to utilize the process of Six Sigma to better meet the needs of your organization.

The Least You Need to Know

- Make Six Sigma project recommendations to display your interest and leadership capabilities.
- Take the initiative to learn more about Six Sigma by studying details about completed projects, researching Six Sigma on the Internet, and reading additional books.

- Use Six Sigma tools in your everyday job to gain experience for taking on larger Six Sigma roles in the future.
- Multiple career paths exist after completing belt projects.

Creative Solutions

In This Chapter

- Designing new processes
- How quick hits can stop the bleeding
- Using the tools outside of Six Sigma projects

Executing DMAIC (define, measure, analyze, improve, and control) projects is not the only way Six Sigma can help companies. From creating new processes to finding quick wins, we show you how Six Sigma can help individuals or teams achieve positive results. This includes the most simple to the most complex business problems.

Creative Solutions

While the DMAIC process works great for improving existing processes, organizations often find the need to create new processes. This approach to Six Sigma is called Design for Six Sigma (DFSS).

The need for a brand new process arises when at least one of the following conditions occurs:

- You have discovered no process exists to produce a product or service to satisfy a new customer need.
- You have several ways to produce an output, none of which are completely accurate.
- You have completely optimized your process but are still not satisfying the customer's needs.

A company might recognize the need to create a new process as a result of the DMAIC analysis phase. In this case, the project team usually has difficulty finding one or two root causes to the problem. Instead, they find many broken pieces, all interrelated. To fix only one or two of the broken pieces would not achieve the benefits desired.

At this point, the project team makes the decision to design a new process. For instance, in the process of restocking blue widgets, we may have found that each operator was following his or her own interpretation of a process, each different and unique and each producing varied results. In this case, DFSS would be used to examine all current processes, and the team would use the components of each to potentially design one single process.

DFSS can also be used when a company is proposing a new product or service. In this case, the company might use it to select the right product or service offering or identify the best method for marketing the new product or service. For instance, when a company decides to add a new product line, it must design a process for how the product will be produced and sold. Or perhaps a company wants to try a new method of marketing to existing customers. The marketing executive might ask, "How do we ensure the new marketing approach will achieve the desired results?" In both of these cases, the DFSS method would be effective in developing and testing a new process.

In another case of selecting DFSS, a process for closing quotes was originally optimized to three days using Six Sigma DMAIC. In other words, the best possible operation of the process took three days to complete. Research showed that in order to satisfy customers completely, the time to close a quote must be one day. To reach this new level of customer satisfaction, the process had to be redesigned using DFSS to meet this new customer requirement.

Process Pointers

DFSS, just like DMAIC, focuses on the customer. Understanding the needs of the customer enables you to design the right process.

Upon completion of the design, DFSS uses validation and control tools similar to DMAIC to ensure the acceptance and survival of the new process. This can be seen most clearly by looking at one of the most popular methodologies used in DFSS called *DMADV* (De-mad-vee). The five phases of DMADV are …

- Define.
- Measure.
- Analyze.
- Design.
- Verify.

The early stages in DMADV are very similar to the early stages of DMAIC, except the last two phases are altered to accommodate the new process being designed. Specifically, the design and control phases of DMAIC are changed to design and verify. Many other methods exist for the design phase of Six Sigma which includes IDOV—*Identify* the opportunity, *Design* a new solution, *Optimize* the solution, *Validate* the solution. Some methods add an additional I for *Implementation*, and others add a final C for *Control*. The basics are simple: *Define* what is needed by the customer; *Explore* the current and potential new processes; *Experiment* to identify the best method; *Optimize* the best found design; *Verify* the new design; *Implement* the new design; and *Control* the new design.

Quick Hits

A common response from executives involved in process improvement projects is "I can't wait several months to fix things. I must have results *now!*" While Six Sigma does not recommend the band-aid approach to sustain improvements long-term, steps are built into the methodology for identifying quick hit solutions resulting in short-term benefits until long-term solutions can be implemented.

The band-aid approach can be explained as thinking you have fixed one part of the process; however, when this process fix is put in place, another part of the process fails. In essence, you have squeezed air from one end of the balloon to the other. The same number of defects may exist, but they are now created in a different location of the process.

Band-aid solutions are usually used to inject the process with a quick improvement that will last just long enough for the team to work with Six Sigma rigor, behind the scenes, to implement a permanent solution to sustain and then exceed the gains of the quick hit or band-aid solution.

The Six Sigma approach to using quick hits allows teams to find solutions to root problems that can be implemented immediately. Quick hits are usually found when a process is being run improperly. The quick hit is an immediate stop to the improper actions. Use this approach to stop the bleeding, and then use Six Sigma to eliminate the cause of the bleeding.

A silly example of applying a band-aid solution is this: Say you get blisters on your heel every time you wear your black high-heeled shoes. The quick hit is to stop wearing your black high-heeled shoes. However, over time, you might find all high-heeled shoes cause this problem. A business example would be excessive wait times in a checkout line of a grocery store. A quick fix might be to open more register lines. This change might produce an immediate reduction in wait times. However, if the sales lift of having more open registers does not cover the cost of the additional cashiers, the improvement will fail and the process will drop back to its original quality level. But, if a long-term solution of automating the checkout process was put in place shortly after the quick hit, a win-win is achieved.

Lessons Learned

We explained earlier that the goal of implementing Six Sigma across an organization is to get as many people as possible understanding the basic methodology and tools of Six Sigma. The primary reason for this is to enable every employee, in every position, to constantly think about making things better. Employees don't have to be black belts or green belts to seek improvements. All they have to do is apply what they know.

The three Six Sigma principles every employee should know are …

- Always focus on the customer.
- Use data to make decisions.
- Plan before action.

So which tools are the most valuable for supporting these principles? Our top-five tools to help encourage employees to partake in continuous corporate improvements would be:

- SIPOC
- Brainstorming
- Charters
- Work plans
- Process maps

Each of the tools is easy to explain and can provide real impact when used alone. For instance, when employees create a SIPOC (Supplier, Inputs, Process, Output, Customer) diagram of their processes, they will immediately understand who their customers are, and they can begin to focus all individual actions toward satisfying those customers.

Brainstorming is valuable to generate new ideas, which are used to make things better. Associates who understand how and when to use brainstorming techniques become better brainstorming session participants and facilitators as well as valued contributors of new ideas.

Charters and work plans provide structure around any task or project an employee is focused on. By understanding the goal of a charter, employees begin to recognize the principles of planning and communication. Likewise, work plans help employees consider all steps involved before taking action.

Lastly, one of our favorite tools, which can be used alone anywhere in the organization, is the process map. As every employee follows certain steps to complete their job, an understanding of process maps will provide insight into which steps might be non–value-added and which steps might be missing in the process.

The Least You Need to Know

- Design for Six Sigma is a technique used to create new processes.
- Quick hits can be used to find short-term solutions, while the long-term solution is underway.
- By sharing the basic principles of Six Sigma across an organization, employees of any position can make improvements.

Chapter 

Going Astray

In This Chapter

- What to do when data is hard to find
- Tips for finding customer requirements
- Why project leads can be defects
- When project champions lose touch

While Six Sigma is a strong methodology for solving business problems, nothing is foolproof. When data can't be found or a project team loses sight of the customer, Six Sigma projects might take a turn for the worse. And when project champions or executive sponsors leave the company, project failure appears imminent.

In this final chapter, we talk about all the things that can go wrong during and after a Six Sigma implementation. We also provide you with strategies an organization can use to dig themselves out of a mess.

Where Art Thou, Data?

Usually, the biggest complaint we hear from young organizations getting started with Six Sigma is, "We don't have enough data to know whether we have problems or, specifically, where the problems are located." Sometimes, a true lack of data does exist and collecting the data would take a project team far outside the recommended project completion timeframe. Other times, the team leading the project just doesn't know where to look.

For organizations that have limited automated systems and reporting, finding data to support the fact that a problem exists and baseline the problem can be a challenge. In some cases, the systems in place are capturing the data at too high a level and system modifications are needed to gather the details required. For instance, imagine a system only collecting sales data at the corporate level because it was implemented before regions existed. If a team's measurement plan requires the collection of sales data by region to determine whether or not differences exist among the regions, the team has two choices:

- Request a modification be made to the system to capture sales data by region.
- Create a manual process to capture the data at the level required.

If a manual process is implemented, additional resources are often required to capture, track, and validate the data. Sometimes, the resources within a project team do not suffice based on the *sample size* required. In addition to resource costs, travel expenses might be incurred based on the location of the data that needs collected.

Sigma Sayings

Sample size is the statistical representation of the population from which conclusions can be drawn.

Waiting for a modification to a current system might impact the overall timeline for the project. Or, a worse-case scenario, the information technology group may not have available resources or the priority to modify the current system.

When this happens, an organization implementing Six Sigma usually sets up data collection methods outside of an established Six Sigma project. This means establishing data priorities for the company and defining methods to collect this data in anticipation of future Six Sigma projects.

Usually, the data requirements are identified as a result of loosely defined corporate metrics. For instance, a CEO wants to reduce the costs of advertising expenditures by 5 percent. Unfortunately, due to a lack of detailed data, the chief marketing officer (CMO) might not have an accurate breakdown of the costs by area to understand which areas to target. Therefore, the CMO might begin a data collection effort to identify the various expense buckets. After the costs are identified, a Six Sigma lead would be assigned to begin a new project aimed at reducing the largest expense buckets to help the CMO achieve the goal.

Defect Alert

Cycle time reduction projects commonly lack detailed data. To baseline this type of project, an organization must be tracking the time it takes to perform each task within the process. An example is the amount of time it takes a customer to go through a checkout line. While this may appear simple enough to measure by standing next to a cashier with a stopwatch and check sheet, it's actually very complicated. The measurement has to take into account such things as the experience levels of the cashier, customer types, store types, transaction types, time of day, and so on. All of these variables increase the necessary sample size required for the measure. Again, measuring this manually could require additional team resources along with additional time built into the measure phase of the project.

Customer Who?

A common problem in Six Sigma occurs when an organization does not know who their customer is or what their customer wants. Too often, teams fail at delighting their customers. They reach a solution and find out, in the end, the solution did not meet the needs of the customer.

Many teams find that collecting customer data can be a costly and time-consuming endeavor, similar to the data collection challenges we just discussed. Imagine the inefficiencies that could exist from multiple project teams spread across the organization all spending money to collect customer data. If this is the external customer and each team is trying to identify customer requirements, the waste could be enormous. For this reason, you will often see organizations create a central mechanism for collecting detailed customer data to satisfy existing and future projects.

One company we worked with to implement Six Sigma began their implementation effort by developing a cohesive Internet survey process to collect feedback related to every area in the business. Input was solicited throughout each functional area, including executive leaders and Six Sigma belts in an effort to identify the type of customer information required. Processes were developed for distributing the survey results as well as maintaining the information over time.

However, when the customer is an internal customer directly related to a specific functional area, the project team is often tasked with collecting customer requirements on his or her own. Examples of internal customers are …

- A sales team for a lead-generating process.
- All employees for a paycheck distribution process.
- Executives for a Six Sigma black belt selection process.

Similar methods are used to gather customer requirements, regardless of whether the customer is internal or external. First, a team must create strong interview questions to determine what customers need. Second, they should develop an efficient method for executing the interview questions. The Internet survey example works great when customers are dispersed and difficult to reach. In some cases, one-on-one interviews are most effective. Focus groups can be used to bring together like customer groups into a common setting with common questions. In many cases, multiple methods for soliciting customer information are used to ensure all requirements are captured successfully.

After a process for collecting the customer data has been established, identifying the right questions to ask and capturing the responses effectively can be challenging. The first thing you need to do is ask questions to help determine what the customer wants. What does the customer expect from us?

This can be by category or service. You then need to see how you are doing relative to those customer wants. For example, a customer calling a call center wants the call center associate to be courteous and efficient. From there, we generate questions to attain performance levels for each of these requirements. This can be done on one survey after external research has been conducted to identify the wants of the customer. Otherwise, it needs to be an interactive, live, or even a two-part survey.

Words, Words, Words

Communication, which on the surface looks to be the easiest part of a Six Sigma project, is usually where we find the most problems. Ineffective communication comes in many shapes and sizes. It includes over-communication, under-communication, wrong types of communication, and even wrong levels of communication.

Over-communication exists when project leads and team members distribute everything to everyone. Instead of targeting the appropriate communication to the appropriate audience, they cut corners by attempting to create common materials that everyone can understand. This never works. For instance, inviting several team members to a meeting via e-mail and copying individuals who are not needed at the meeting shows that you are not organized, and potentially wasting the time of others.

Conversely, we've seen teams fail as a result of under-communicating. As we mentioned previously, when associates, executives, or other groups touching the process are left out of the loop, it is a lot harder to get them to accept changes. In addition, key points affecting the process changes might be missed. For example, when the Six Sigma team decided to modify the ordering process of blue widgets, they worked with procurement, but they did not include logistics. Hence, when procurement made the order changes, the logistics model was not changed, and the company ended up paying for unutilized shipping, as a result of the procurement team ordering less without the logistics team reducing the shipping needs.

Holding meetings to disburse one-way communication or sending written communication when trying to solicit feedback are common mistakes we see. For instance, it is usually unnecessary to conduct a meeting with an extended or secondary team only to provide a status update. However, if you want to solicit feedback on a proposed process with this extended team, e-mailing a process map and list of questions is usually not effective.

Clear communication is a direct function of the audience for the communication. If a document using Six Sigma jargon is sent to associates that have not yet been to a Six Sigma class, the communication will appear unclear and useless. If the same document is sent to a master black belt, the document might receive high praise. A project team must know the audience receiving the communication. In addition, the audience dictates the level of detail to provide. Most executives do not want to know the steps a team took to identify possible solutions. Instead, they want to know the alternatives, the recommended solution, and the costs and benefits associated with the solution. A master black belt, on the other hand, will want to know that the appropriate tools were utilized to define the alternatives and select the right solution.

Process Pointers

Creating an extended team in addition to a core team can provide additional feedback and perspective the core team might overlook. An extended team can usually be brought in less frequently to approve or disapprove of the direction of a project. Use this team to validate findings prior to the completion and execution of a tollgate review.

Starting Too Small

Many companies refuse to take into account the strong cultural change required across a company to achieve benefits from Six Sigma. Instead, they choose to implement Six Sigma only within one area in the company or attempt to start with a pilot and make the determination to expand based on the pilot results. These methods of implementing Six Sigma fail for so many reasons.

First, implementing Six Sigma in only one area of the business defies the top-down approach and support required to make Six Sigma successful. When projects are not centered on key corporate metrics, resources will not be attained and support for the project will not exist.

In addition, these approaches suggest that business processes are confined to one functional area. We know this is not true. For example, if a team is tasked with improving a cashier's check-approval process, the operations group, financial audit team, training organization, and probably the information systems group all require involvement to be successful. If these groups don't have an understanding of Six Sigma, the project is likely to fail.

Lastly, when resources are assigned to projects without effective mentoring and training, failure will occur. What companies find when implementing Six Sigma in one area is they are unable to justify the training and mentoring costs. For instance, suppose only two to three black belt positions are created within the finance group of an organization. While external training might be utilized for this group, finding external training classes targeted at finance process owners, team members, and general finance associates is usually more difficult. As you recall, training curriculum focused on the type of business with real-life examples is the most effective. Alternately, the cost of hiring one master black belt to support this small number of black belts might be unjustifiable.

If the organization we discussed is expecting to use the results from the finance implementation as a justification to implement Six Sigma everywhere, they may never realize the return as the finance projects will absorb the costs disproportionately.

If the legal department used Six Sigma to find a way to reduce fines for excessive alarms, the operations team may not be able to understand or implement similar solutions due to the fact that they do not understand the methodology for implementing sustainable solutions.

As Time Goes On

During the first two years of most Six Sigma implementations, companies experience sweeping changes resulting in large financial results and increased customer satisfaction. But, after the honeymoon is over, companies sometimes find the results begin to slide.

When a Six Sigma implementation begins, problems are usually stacked high for a company. Selecting the priority projects becomes the challenge because there are so many problems to fix. The first round of belts usually get to bite off the low-hanging fruit as they focus on the obvious things that need to be fixed. Usually, strong data exists showing holes in quality and major points of customer dissatisfaction. When the following waves of belts hit, sometime between the second and third year, finding the areas of dissatisfaction and low quality become more challenging. These projects typically require larger measure phases to pinpoint the problems.

Corporate goals and strategies can also change over time. When this occurs, some projects may be put on hold or even replaced with other projects of a higher priority. Many factors can cause abrupt changes to corporate goals and strategy, such as changes in the marketplace, competitor environment, political upheaval, and economic influences. Whatever the cause, a Six Sigma organization must be flexible to respond to the changes, even if it means throwing out project work.

The Wrong Leads

As with most people-led initiatives, leaders can make or break a project. Six Sigma projects can crack when leads don't master the tool set, leave the company in the middle of a project, or don't respect their teams.

Sometimes, no matter how great a selection process is, one or two defects seem to emerge. The defect in the case of a belt selection process is an ineffective project lead. Sometimes, this materializes directly after training when the lead displays the inability to understand the material. Often, failure to apply the material becomes evident during tollgate reviews. In some instances, project team members provide feedback to a project sponsor or master black belt alerting them of the issues the lead is creating.

Regardless of how the defect is found, eliminating the defect is critical. Without the right leader guiding a team with the right toolset, the best solution is unlikely to be identified. In fact, the solution implemented might produce more defects in the end.

Defect Alert

An ineffective team lead can create low morale on a team resulting in a negative impact on the project process.

But how does an organization fix the problem of selecting a poor project lead? Just as with any employee placed in the wrong position, the appropriate performance action plan must be instituted. However, most organizations address personnel issues on an annual basis. Because of the scope of changes a project lead can affect and the relatively short duration of projects, sometimes waiting a year is not an option. Alternatives are …

- Provide additional training and closely monitor the lead.
- Develop an action plan to develop the lead.
- Create a shadowing plan, wherein the project lead is shadowed by an existing master black belt.

When a lead leaves a company during the middle of a project, the impact on the project team can be devastating. If the supervisor of the lead knows in advance of the departure, they can usually assign another belt to the project and have an opportunity for the new belt to spend time with the departing belt.

If the departure is abrupt, a team member might be able to assist in getting another belt up to speed. In addition, if the documentation is kept current, another belt can easily take the lead.

The Missing Champ

The most common cause we've seen for Six Sigma projects and implementations going astray is the lack of continued involvement from a project champion. An organization expects a project champion to …

- Speak the language.
- Have metrics and goals tied to Six Sigma successes.
- Provide the best resources for participation.
- Know how to define and scope projects.
- Provide support and buy-in and eliminate roadblocks.
- Know how to measure project success.

When a project champion fails to achieve any one of these expectations, entire Six Sigma implementations can fail.

One misunderstanding is that the master black belt is responsible for driving the project lead to success. It is the job of the champion to drive the black belt to success, while the master black belt is the guide through the methodology and acts as an agent for the black belt to get the most out of the champion and the project.

A lack of champion involvement can begin with the selection of a project that doesn't match company goals. Champions with a limited understanding of Six Sigma, who are mandated to get a project going, might suggest projects out of line with company strategy. This results in difficulty acquiring the necessary resources to achieve success. For instance, if technology is required to improve the process and the information technology group has other priorities, the project timeline can be affected negatively.

Even when the right project is selected and scoped, if the project champion is hard to reach, fails to attend meetings, or simply refuses to stay involved, a project can lose resources or reach conclusions that conflict with other things happening in the organization.

So, what causes project champions to disappear? Sometimes, champions leave a company and the replacement either has a restricted understanding of Six Sigma or has other priorities as a new member of the executive leadership team. This often leaves the project lead floundering to both train the new champion and keep the project moving.

The Least You Need to Know

- To minimize depleting data collection resources, collection efforts should be coordinated across projects.
- Capturing the wrong customer requirements can lead to inappropriate project results.
- Ineffective project leads can cause projects to fail.
- When project champions leave a company, projects can be negatively impacted.

Appendix A

Sigma Values

The following table enables you to convert a process yield to a Sigma value.

Sigma	% Good	DPMO
0.1	**0.0807567**	**919243**
0.2	0.0968005	903199
0.3	0.1150697	884930
0.4	0.1356661	864334
0.5	0.1586553	841345
0.6	0.1840601	815940
0.7	0.2118553	788145
0.8	0.2419636	758036
0.9	0.2742531	725747
1.0	**0.3085375**	**691462**
1.1	0.3445783	655422
1.2	0.3820886	617911
1.3	0.4207403	579260
1.4	0.4601721	539828
1.5	0.5000000	500000
1.6	0.5398279	460172

continues

continued

Sigma	% Good	DPMO
1.7	0.5792597	420740
1.8	0.6179114	382089
1.9	0.6554217	344578
2.0	**0.6914625**	**308538**
2.1	0.7257469	274253
2.2	0.7580364	241964
2.3	0.7881447	211855
2.4	0.8159399	184060
2.5	0.8413447	158655
2.6	0.8643339	135666
2.7	0.8849303	115070
2.8	0.9031995	96801
2.9	0.9192433	80757
3.0	**0.9331928**	**66807**
3.1	0.9452007	54799
3.2	0.9554346	44565
3.3	0.9640697	35930
3.4	0.9712835	28716
3.5	0.9772499	22750
3.6	0.9821356	17864
3.7	0.9860966	13903
3.8	0.9892759	10724
3.9	0.9918025	8198
4.0	**0.9937903**	**6210**
4.1	0.9953388	4661
4.2	0.9965330	3467
4.3	0.9974448	2555

Sigma	% Good	DPMO
4.4	0.9981341	1866
4.5	0.9986500	1350
4.6	0.9990323	968
4.7	0.9993128	687
4.8	0.9995165	483
4.9	0.9996630	337
5.0	**0.9997673**	**233**
5.1	0.9998409	159
5.2	0.9998922	108
5.3	0.9999276	72.4
5.4	0.9999519	48.1
5.5	0.9999683	31.7
5.6	0.9999793	20.7
5.7	0.9999866	13.4
5.8	0.9999915	8.5
5.9	0.9999946	5.4
6.0	**0.9999966**	**3.4**

Glossary

baseline A historical measurement of the current process output that may be used as a comparison with customer expectations.

black belt A full-time Six Sigma project leader.

cause-and-effect diagram A visual tool used to display relationships between variables.

change management Planning for acceptance around a new process or organizational change, which will ultimately affect people.

consensus building The process of gaining agreement among multiple team members usually with the help of a mediator. The mediator might present pros and cons for each side of the conflict.

contingency plans Detailed plans specifying alternative actions to take if something in the implemented solution goes wrong.

control chart A chart used to identify patterns over time.

Critical to Quality Characteristics (CTQs) The specific things that are critical to quality in customers' minds.

customer A customer is someone receiving the output or end result of your process.

customer specification A goal or requirement set by the customer based on the customer's needs.

data stratification The process of dividing data into smaller groups based on factors identified by the project team. This could lead a project team to focus its work on a specific subgroup of the population.

defect An error or mistake resulting in reduced customer satisfaction.

Design for Six Sigma (DFSS) A Six Sigma approach to defining and designing a brand new process.

Design of Experiment (DOE) A tool used to combine multiple factors and test the effects of these factors on a process.

DMAIC The most commonly used Six Sigma methodology. It consists of five sequential phases: define, measure, analyze, improve, and control. The DMAIC process is primarily applied when problems occur within an existing process.

effective listening The ability to comprehend what someone else is trying to say. A strong listener focuses directly on the speaker, waits until the speaker has finished making his point, and asks questions to ensure understanding of the speaker's point.

facilitated session A meeting, led by a facilitator, usually including several people pulled together to accomplish a common goal. For instance, a facilitated session might be used to map out a current business process.

Failure Mode and Effect Analysis (FMEA) A tool used to analyze all potential ways a process might fail, along with why the process might fail.

frequency plot A plot that shows how often an event occurs.

green belt A part-time Six Sigma project lead usually focusing on smaller projects while performing another job in the company. A green belt is usually assigned to fix problems within the functional area to which they report.

hard-dollar savings Expenses eliminated from companies' budgets, such as reduced payroll expenses or reduced energy costs.

Hawthorn Effect Positive results seen from making a change to the environment of the associates. Based on the early quality studies of Hawthorn, improved results were seen in sewing factories by simply turning up the brightness of the factory lights. No significant change was made to the process, but the process improved. Over time, the quality level of the factory returned to its normal low production levels.

hypothesis testing The method of using tools, such as ANOVA, t-test, Chi-Square, and proportions tests, to determine whether a true difference exists between two groups.

lean Sigma A term adopted from Motorola's lean manufacturing that focuses on eliminating waste. Waste is defined as a loss of productivity, safety, inventory, and so on.

master black belt A full-time trainer of Six Sigma usually responsible for overseeing the implementation of Six Sigma throughout the organization.

measurement plan A document describing the specific measuring tool, including instructions on how the tool will be used, and a list of who will use the tool.

pareto chart A pareto chart shows how often an event occurs across various categories.

performance development plan A document used by many companies to specify additional skills and knowledge components necessary to enhance an associate's work performance.

process A string of actions focused toward a goal or end result. Examples of processes include: cooking dinner, answering a phone, or building airplanes.

process owner The person with direct responsibility for the production of an output.

project champion An executive leader responsible for setting and maintaining project direction and overall engagement throughout the project lifecycle.

Pugh Matrix A tool to assist teams in finding the best solution to a problem.

root cause The most fundamental reason for a defect occurring repeatedly. When a root cause is removed, the defect is eliminated.

sample size The statistical representation of the population from which conclusions can be drawn.

scatter plots A tool used to show relationships between two factors.

Six Sigma A management philosophy used to solve business problems adopted throughout all areas of an organization. The term Six Sigma also refers to a quality measure (that is, 3.4 defects per 1 million chances or opportunities is 6.0 Sigma). The fewer defects produced, the higher Sigma level achieved.

stakeholder analysis A listing of all key people who may touch the current or future process in any way, shape, or form, along with the type of communication required for each.

statistically significant A result that differs from the basis enough to suggest that the difference between the two is not by accident.

statistics A mathematical system used to understand a population of data by analyzing a sample or small portion of the data.

tollgates Scheduled meetings with project sponsors occurring at specific stages throughout the project to present clear project definitions, current findings, and future direction of the project.

tree diagrams A visual tool used to display relationships between variables.

variation The occurrence of something happening that was different from that which was expected. This is the fluctuation in the process output, or the spread of data around the process mean, sometimes called *noise*.

work-out sessions A type of meeting consisting of people with knowledge about a particular process often used to help formulate solutions to a problem occurring within the process. Usually a session leader is present to keep the discussion on target. Sign-off on best-guess solutions usually ends the session.

Index

D

F

G

H-I

J-K-L

M

N-O

P

Q

R

S

T–U

V-W

X-Y-Z